INTRODUCING

BLACK THEOLOGY
OF LIBERATION

INTRODUCING

BLACK THEOLOGY OF LIBERATION

Dwight N. Hopkins

ORBIS BOOKS

Maryknoll, New York 10545

The Catholic Foreign Mission Society of America (Maryknoll) recruits and trains people for overseas missionary service. Through Orbis Books, Maryknoll aims to foster the international dialogue that is essential to mission. The books published, however, reflect the opinions of their authors and are not meant to represent the official position of the society.

To obtain more information about Maryknoll or Orbis Books, please visit our website at www.maryknoll.org.

Published by Orbis Books, Maryknoll, NY 10545-0308.

Manufactured in the United States of America

Library of Congress Cataloging-in-Publication Data
Hopkins, Dwight N.
    Introducing Black theology of liberation / Dwight N. Hopkins.
        p.   cm.
    Includes bibliographical references and index.
    ISBN 1-57075-286-9 (pbk.)
    1. Black theology.   2. Womanist theology.   3. Liberation theology.
I. Title.   II. Title: Black theology of liberation.
BT82.7.H67   1999
230'.089'96073–dc21   99-38798

For

My wife: Linda E. Thomas—
a balm in Gilead

My daughter: Eva Shirley Hopkins—
a spiritual light for the twenty-first century

My mother: Dora H. Hopkins—
an intellectual thirst for all times

Contents

Acknowledgments

Many persons and institutions have nurtured me in my vocation as a theologian.

Churches: Cedar Street Memorial Baptist Church (Richmond, Virginia; Benjamin E. Robertson Sr., senior pastor); Bethany Baptist Church (Brooklyn, New York; William Augustus Jones, senior pastor); Allen Temple Baptist Church (Oakland, California; J. Alfred Smith Sr., senior pastor); Trinity United Church of Christ (Chicago; Jeremiah A. Wright Jr., senior pastor); and St. Mark United Methodist Church (Chicago; Myron McCoy, senior pastor).

Schools: the intellectually stimulating, black-pride affirming, and segregated public elementary schools in Richmond, Virginia; five years at Groton Preparatory School (an all-boys boarding school in Groton, Massachusetts); Harvard University; Union Theological Seminary (New York City); and the University of Cape Town (Cape Town, South Africa).

Family: family members in Richmond, Virginia; Oakland, California; Baltimore, Maryland; and Guguletu, Cape Town, South Africa.

I have lectured on black theology of liberation throughout the United States and South Africa, at the American Academy of Religion, at the Ecumenical Association of Third World Theologians, and at different churches.

I want to thank the students who took my classes at Santa Clara University (Santa Clara, California) and who now take my courses at the University of Chicago Divinity School (especially students who take my three-part sequence throughout the year — black theology, the first generation; black theology, the

second generation; and black theology and womanist theology
in dialogue, which is cotaught with my wife, Linda E. Thomas).
Thanks to W. Clark Gilpin, dean of the University of Chicago
Divinity School, for his initial and consistent support for my
intellectual projects.

Special thanks to certain individuals who have, over the
years, debated with me, challenged me, and pushed me intellectually: James H. Cone, Will Coleman, George C. L. Cummings,
and James A. Noel. In addition to that group, the following gave sharp criticisms of certain parts of the manuscript
of this book: Gayraud S. Wilmore, Kelly Brown Douglas, and
Emilie M. Townes.

Thanks to Robert Ellsberg of Orbis Books for his support,
critiques, and patience.

As noted above, my wife, Linda E. Thomas, and I coteach a
course on womanist theology and black theology in conversation. We teach two versions of this course, one at the University
of Chicago Divinity School and one at Garrett-Evangelical
Theological Seminary (Evanston, Illinois). To our knowledge,
this is the first time such a course has been taught. We have
co-lectured on black theology and womanist theology in South
Africa and at schools in the United States. We have co-authored
articles on the same topic. We continue to nurture each other
about our vocations: faith, family, service, education, and healing. I also give my profound thanks to her for co-authoring the
chapter on womanist theology in the present book.

Introduction

Black people in America have survived and thrived with a spirit of hope and determination. Even with 100 million of their African ancestors stolen from the Continent, 246 years of slavery, 100 years of legal segregation, and decades of de facto oppression, something has kept them on a path toward freedom. A way of holding on to this something has been passed down from generation to generation.

At times, it has seemed as if no one could help them or no way could be found to explain why one people had suffered perhaps more and longer than any other race on earth. That is why they sang, "Sometimes I feel like a motherless child, a long way from home." This ongoing feeling of being at home but not at home, even in the present period, has something to do with the sinister and seductive split forced upon them by the suspicious gaze of the larger white world and by an internal ache that often gnaws at the very sinews of their hearts.

They have suffered this frustrating instinct and grotesque insanity for no other reason than their skin color. They have tried to answer this demonic dilemma by asking, "Why Lord?" They have fought in every war in this "New World" — from the first massacres of Native Americans, to the War of Independence against the British, up to the latest aggressive skirmishes in foreign lands. Some have made it to the highest military ranks, including the commander of the Joint Chiefs of Staff.

In the United States, they have consistently voted in higher numbers than other racial and ethnic groups, often providing the winning margins in presidential elections. Even the small black upper-middle class have shown their competitive muscle, despite the presence of a glass ceiling in all areas of American society. But racism — benign and malignant, conservative and liberal — has acted like a wound deep within their psyches.

Blues singers have wailed about the pain: "The man I'm gonna marry ain't been born yet, / and his momma done died long ago." Enslaved African American musical artists have moaned the suffering: "I've been 'buked and I've been scorned." They have tried to turn around the absurdity of their existence by mocking ditties: "If you white, you all right.... / If you black, get back, get way back!" Black consciousness poets of the 1960s responded by pushing a religious critique through a nationalist contempt: "The white man's got a God complex." The potency of pain and the persistence of the predicament are as definite as the sun rising tomorrow morning. The negative repercussions of racial difference continue to haunt American culture. Yet there has persisted and remains today a spirit that moves African Americans — in spite of.

Black people in the United States have always had faith in a power that would sustain them through struggle and aid them in their movement to become full human beings. It has been and remains a belief that this world of racism was not the final word over their will to survive. This spirit possessed Africans wrapped in chains as they hurled their black bodies over the sides of slave ships because they preferred to die laughing in the mouths of circling sharks rather than to live in shackles. Others began an insurrection to support the British when the thirteen colonies fought for white people's independence while still maintaining black slavery.

Frederick Douglass let forth this spirit when he called the founding documents of the new United States of America rag sheets. In less biting ways, this spirit empowered some blacks to enter the electoral arena. And on any Sunday morning at eleven A.M., you can hear this spirit infusing the message of black preachers who, in a comical but prophetic way, urge their African American congregations that a God of liberation will deliver them just as sure as Yahweh delivered from the fiery furnace "Shadrach, Meshach, and 'A-Bad-Negro.'"

At the same time, the winds of this spirit have intensified the flames of urban rebellions. Or this spirit has often simply descended upon a person and made him or her shout, moan, or rock back and forth as solitary signs that there is something on the inside of that individual that the world didn't give and that the world can't take away. The external world of racism and the internal world of hurting will not and cannot have the final say.

This spirit of liberation, unpredictable and untamed, has gripped the African American collective psyche since 1619, the creation time of the new race of people called Negars, coloreds, Negroes, Afro-Americans, blacks, and African Americans. That spirit was behind the black women's club movement when it sought to lift up the entire Negro people at the beginning of the twentieth century. W. E. B. Du Bois felt some of its power while organizing Pan-African movements. Marcus Garvey channeled some of this spirit of liberation to the roughly two and a half million members of his Universal Negro Improvement Association.

More recently, the musical group Sweet Honey in the Rock kept civil rights workers inspired by blowing the songs of this spirit into the struggle for "freedom now." Over two million African American men pledged to work for atonement, accountability, and individual and collective black freedom at the Million Man March, a pledge based on this spirit. And the most institutionalized expression of spirit preaching and spirit praying and spirit resisting is found in the black Christian church.

Definition

Indeed, though the spirit of liberation, in multiple manifestations, has permeated African Americans' presence and powered their persistence at being black in the world, African American faith has found its most enduring entrenchment in the black Christian church. Yet a clear faith of freedom has not always been the dominant trend in black reality, even in the church. The black church's claims that it believes in and works with a God of liberation have not always squared with its action. Different spirits exist. But how does one know if the nature of the faith and the demonstration of a practice of freedom are in line with the spirit of liberation? A black theology of liberation aids the resolution of this inconsistency.

In the context of the African American church, black theology considers the following question: What does it mean to be black and Christian for a people situated in the midst of American racism and called by God to be full human beings? Black theology believes that the God of freedom has created African Americans to be free — to reach their full humanity without obstacles blocking the goal of becoming human beings who can freely do God's will. And through Jesus Christ's liberation message and presence, God has provided a way for the church to move toward that freedom. Similarly, God today continues to offer a divine Spirit to enable and sustain black folk on their journey toward a liberated humanity.

Black theology works with African American churches so that they will remain responsible to this divine calling. Christianity and the church represent institutional manifestations of belief. Theology serves as a critical conscience of the church's vocation to liberate the poor in their journey with God to full humanity. To believe in and witness to faith require the ongoing critical questioning about whether or not that belief and witness are in line with the God of liberation of the oppressed. Black theology carries out this function.

Black theology, therefore, is an effort of African American people to claim their blackness and their freedom as people of God. Freedom comes when black poor folk, led by the African American church, live out their freedom because God helps them in their daily struggle against personal pain and collective oppression. This is what Martin Luther King Jr. taught black theology. In addition, a liberation movement needs to free black minds from self-hate and subordination to white power. Malcolm X preached this lesson when he said to his African American audience: the greatest tragedy of black people is when they accept the standards of white beauty and actively avoid their black and African cultures.

Today race still matters in the United States. W. E. B. Du Bois's profound words continue to echo throughout the land — the problem of the century remains the color line, the color line for poor and working-class black folk.[1] To be an African American means an experience of antiblack racism.[2] But it also means the joy and beauty of celebrating the intellectual and spiritual gifts of black folk.[3]

Therefore, to be black and Christian together is to accept a specific calling — that is, to struggle against forces that would block being black in the world and against the obstacles preventing African Americans from achieving their full individual and group humanity, which God has created them to reach. At the same time, and even more importantly, it means having faith in a movement for individual and systemic liberation, a liberation that is the final work that God and oppressed people will carry out to bring about a full humanity. Black theology recognizes that God, through Jesus Christ and the presence of the Holy Spirit, works with the poor as they learn to love themselves enough to practice their total freedom and create their full humanity on earth as it is in heaven.

In summary, the Christian part of black theology states that the God of freedom, through the birth, life, death, and resurrection of Jesus Christ the liberator, has provided a journey of faith and hope to be free. Now God's Spirit of liberation offers empowerment to the oppressed African American community to struggle for the full realization of that community's structural and personal free humanity. It is God's will for the oppressed to be free of racism and become a fully created people of God. This is what it means to be black and Christian. And a black theology of liberation works to keep the church and the community accountable to that claim.

Purpose

This book is an introduction to *black theology as a prophetic theology of liberation.* It examines the relation between the black experience and a faith in God as the liberator of that experience. Specifically for African Americans, to be a Christian is to identify with the freedom stories (e.g., in the book of Exodus) of the Hebrew slaves fleeing from Egyptian bondage. It is proclaiming Jesus' public sermon of liberation of the voiceless and emancipation of the downtrodden (e.g., Luke 4:18ff.). And it is to receive the final reward of a full humanity for those who have believed in and practiced God's will of justice for the marginalized (e.g., Matt. 25:31ff.). Therefore, for a black theology of liberation, if the African American church is a true follower of the Way of Jesus and truly surrenders to the empowerment of the divine Spirit, then its work is to help build on earth God's new Common Wealth for the poor — those who are both materially without wealth and spiritually poor. *Introducing Black Theology of Liberation* examines the dimensions of that process.

This book argues that the unique contribution of black theology is discovering the core message of personal and structural liberation in the Hebrew and Christian Scriptures and connecting this message with God's presence in African Americans' movement for justice. This interpretation and practice present black theology as perhaps the first form of an American radical Christian theology. Black theology of liberation arose from the black church as a Christian movement for the transformation of personal and systemic power-relations in American society.

It came out of the effort to affirm God's positive relation to poor African American people and to defend against white supremacy. But its influence is not limited to black people. It also impacts the way traditional theology is done throughout the world.

So it is good news to be black and Christian — not only in the United States, but all over the earth. People of African descent in Africa, Asia, Latin America, the Caribbean, the Pacific Islands, North America, and Europe are celebrating liberation as the core of the gospel story.[4] As this book argues for the *liberation* essence of black theology, it joins this ongoing global movement for the freedom of the oppressed and, therefore, of all humanity. If the majority of the people in the world who are materially and spiritually oppressed are also free, then this offers hope to remove the unjust power of the minority groups which control most of the world's resources. Removing the internal and external "demons" keeping the majority of the world's population in slavery will help change the structural system of global monopolization by a few. By following the liberation stories in the Bible, the prophetic stand of black theology, and the radical tradition of black church leadership, the African American church has more of a possibility to make a contribution to the practice of freedom for all humanity across the world.

Stages in the Development of Black Theology

The first stage of black theology in the United States began on July 31, 1966.[5] On that day, the National Committee of Negro Churchmen (NCNC — an ad hoc group of African American clergy) published a full-page statement in the *New York Times*.[6] This theological manifesto or Christian declaration was the first attempt in U.S. history to relate the gospel of Jesus to the black community's need for power. The thesis of the statement was that for too long white people had been exercising power without morality while blacks had been practicing a morality without power. This group of African American pastors were responding to new issues in the civil rights struggle.

A month or so earlier, on June 16, 1966, in Greenwood, Mississippi, the black power challenge had come forth from black students in the civil rights movement. Now, what did black power have to do with theology for African American churches? If theology served to make churches accountable to the core message of the Bible, then how could one reconcile the movement of black liberation raised by the black power and black consciousness efforts with Jesus Christ's birth, life, death, and resurrection?

In March 1969, three years after the NCNC publication, James H. Cone published his classic *Black Theology and Black Power*,[7] which combined Martin Luther King Jr.'s demand for the church to be a radical institution for individual and social change with Malcolm X's call for African American people to love their beautiful black selves. Basing its arguments on the lessons of Martin and Malcolm, Cone's book concluded that the movement for black folk to exercise their power in white America was not the opposite of the good news of Jesus Christ. In fact, the struggle for liberation was a key example of Jesus' liberation message for all poor people. In other words, carrying out God's call for personal and collective freedom demanded working toward the freedom of the oppressed African American community. And this faithful practice had universal implications for all people who are marginalized and at the bottom of society.

Restated, Cone's text stated that if the gospel is liberation and Jesus Christ is always in the midst of a liberation struggle, then the liberation movement of black power was the gospel message of twentieth-century America. The book charged the black church to make itself accountable to that statement. In stage one of black theology's development, Cone's book provided an answer for African American Christians who were grappling with the question of whether it was possible to be both black and Christian if the gospel of Jesus Christ (as whites defined the Bible) denied black people power as well as a strong sense of their own cultural roots.

This first stage of black theology included debates between radical African American clergy and their white colleagues in Christian churches. At the same time, these African American pastors were trying to develop aspects of a new black theology for the African American church. They believed that the black power and black consciousness movements of the late 1960s revealed the presence of Jesus Christ the liberator. Furthermore, they stated that the essence of Christianity was deliverance of the African American community and freedom for all the oppressed on earth.

The appearance of the National Committee of Negro Churchmen marked the organizational beginnings of stage one of black theology. In this period, African American clergy, administrators, and educators attempted to separate the theological reflection and practice of black religion from those of the conservative and liberal theologies of the white churches. Black theology emerged both as a critique of white conservative theology's rejection of the role of the black church in the civil rights movement and as a critique of white liberal theology's denial of the relation between black religion and black power. In contrast to the various perspectives of white theologians, pastors, and church administrators, black pastors proclaimed liberation of the oppressed as the central thread throughout the Christian good news. For the founders of black theology, the birth, words, life, and resurrection of Jesus Christ were not neutral; they concerned power — those with it and those without.

The creation of the Society for the Study of Black Religion in 1970 marked black theology's transformation into stage two. In this stage, black theology became an academic discipline in which black religious scholars emphasized religious arguments and debates among themselves. More African American scholars had been allowed into divinity schools and seminaries. During this time, African American theologians struggled over issues such as the relation between liberation and reconciliation, God's goodness and human suffering, African religion and black theology, and the spontaneous faith expressions of African American people versus the rigid theological systems of the white academy. Though an academic emphasis characterizes this phase, various historic black church hierarchies also began to respond favorably in an open or quiet way to diverse doctrines of black theology.[8]

Stage three gave birth to the Black Theology Project (1975), which was made up of church persons, community activists, and scholars, with a strong connection between African Americans and the Third World (i.e., Africa, Asia, the Caribbean, and Latin America). The broad range of participants in this new group reflected black theology's turn toward liberation theologies in the Third World. During this stage, black theology also examined forms of African socialism, the day-to-day survival issues in the African American community, black theology's relation to the black church, and the importance of feminism and Marxism.

The first three phases of black theology developed under the pioneering leadership of the first generation of pastors and professors.

The fourth and present stage commenced around the middle of the 1980s and involves a second generation of black religious scholars and pastors. These thinkers emphasize an exploration of theology from any and all aspects of black life and, most strikingly, the exciting challenge of womanists (black female religious scholars and pastors), who have pressed for a holistic black theology that includes race, class, gender, sexual orientation, and ecological issues. Womanists have also demonstrated the urgency of doing black theology from such innovative sources as black fiction and women's roles in the Bible. Womanists have challenged the black church with this question: If 70 to 80 percent of its membership is women, instead of saying the "black church," shouldn't it be called the "black women's church"?

Moreover, this fourth stage shows black theology deepening its ties in both the black church and the academy. The number of African Americans attending graduate schools of divinity, theology, and religion is slowly increasing, and these young scholars are institutionalizing themselves in the American Academy of Religion, the national organization of all scholars with some form of Ph.D. related to religion. Likewise, the Society for the Study of Black Religion remains a vibrant intellectual group for African American religious scholars.

The ties between the African American church and the black scholar have deepened with more professors either pastoring or co-pastoring churches, or working in and with churches in some other capacity. Also, more pastors are entering seminaries and theological and divinity schools to study and develop black theology. Various graduate schools (e.g., Garrett-Evangelical Theological Seminary, Candler School of Theology, Colgate Rochester Divinity School, and Vanderbilt University) have centers on the church and the black experience, furthering the structural relationship between black professors and pastors, on the one hand, and black laypersons, on the other.

Furthermore, the present stage has seen more research and publications which center on primary sources in African American culture and politics, for instance, in the areas of slave narratives, folk tales, music, biography, public policy. Afrocentrism is adding its mark to African American theological concerns today, and it cuts across all particular disciplines in religious studies. In addition, the first generation of black scholars continues to publish texts that are pacesetting in many areas.

Finally, a small group of black Christian educators and ministers are openly establishing their lesbian and gay identities as gifts from God and are, therefore, directly challenging the black

church and black theological beliefs about liberation. Moreover, whatever the contributions of various African American
theologians, today's phase of black theology finds stronger relations between professors and the black church and a more
conscious attempt by black pastors and churches to practice
black theology.

Theological Developments

To deepen our introduction to the current state of black theology (e.g., what it means to be black and Christian), this book
examines six broad areas relevant to the process of doing black
theology. Chapter 1 offers four fundamental building blocks in
the development of a black theology of liberation: slave religion,
a rereading of the Bible, the 1960s black theology movement,
and theological method. Chapter 2 takes a closer look at the
fine distinctions between two wings of the first generation of
black theologians — the political and cultural.

Chapter 3 introduces the second generation of black theologians and outlines the broad areas of religious studies which
they are pioneering based on the theological foundations laid
by the first generation. This chapter concludes with a set of
pointed challenges to the second generation because it faces a
threatening possibility of selling out the interests of the gospel
message and the best interests of the black church. Chapter 4
presents the critical engagement of faith and witness (theology
and ethics) by womanists — African American female religious
scholars. They affirm their unique response to God's calling of
liberation while, simultaneously, distinguishing themselves from
the sexism of black (and white) men and the racism of white
women (and men).

Chapter 5 sums up the historical and current global dialogues in which black theology of liberation is participating.
Black theologians' conversation with liberation theologians in

Africa, Asia, the Caribbean, Latin America, and the Pacific Islands has revealed theological commonalities and differences and has brought into relief the prospects for future conversation and joint activities. The conclusion to the present work summarizes the argument and ends with an outline of areas that black theology must pursue today if it is to answer the question: What does it mean to be black and Christian?

Perhaps twenty-first-century developments in black theology and in the African American church movement will deal more comprehensively with the ways in which the good news of liberation informs all aspects of the African American church and community — the spiritual, material, psychological, economic, cultural, linguistic, political, and the everyday. Still, the vocation of black theology, the black church, and those concerned about the least in society will remain the gospel of full humanity for the poor and a new heaven and new earth for all of creation. *Introducing Black Theology of Liberation* is one contribution in this quest.

Chapter 1

The Development of Black Theology

This chapter introduces the four basic building blocks that were used to construct a black theology of liberation in response to the question, What does it mean to be black and Christian?

First, this chapter examines the historical context of slavery. In this period (1619–1865), enslaved African and African American workers created a new faith called black religion for the oppressed and the poor.

The second important ingredient of black theology of liberation is its unique way of reading and experiencing the Bible. In that book, poor people experienced the theme of exodus, the message of the prophets, and the life of Jesus as the way to freedom. This reinterpretation of scriptures began during the time of slavery but has continued to the present.

Although black theology is rooted historically in slavery and influenced profoundly by a new reading of the Bible, its most important source was developments during the 1950s, 1960s, and early 1970s. In this period, black theology emerged as an effort to relate the gospel to the experiences of the African American freedom struggle and the particular challenge of black power. During this time, black churches and community activists met a God of liberation working closely with those black folk who dared fight for their natural and God-given human rights. In the course of elaborating this new interpretation of the gospel, African American theologians and clergy gradually came to see

15

themselves not as creating something brand new but as developing themes and organizing a style of faith and spirituality that had much deeper roots in the history of the black church and of the overall African American community. In addition, this way of doing theology recovered a prophetic and liberating faith that was rooted in the foundations of Christianity itself.

Finally, this chapter examines the fourth building block of the black theology of liberation: method. The final section thus deals with how conclusions about Jesus Christ are systematically related to the movement for liberation of and among the oppressed, especially the African American poor.

Black Religion during the Slavery Period

Poor black folk created their own faith in the hell of over two hundred years of slavery. Despite being the private property of slave masters, despite being torn from their African homeland and ripped away from parents and other family members, African Americans enjoyed the beauty of a faith which maintained their humanity and their hope in a new heaven and a new earth for their children.

From the seventeenth to nineteenth century, African and African American enslaved workers constructed a new religion drawing on three sources — memories of African religious beliefs, commonsense wisdom from everyday life, and a reinterpretation of the white-supremacy Christianity introduced to them by their Christian slave masters. The cornerstone of a black theology of liberation was thus a slave religion of freedom.

More specifically, working from these three original sources, enslaved African Americans forged the foundational outlines of a black theology within the "Invisible Institution," a name given to the secret times and spaces where blacks worshiped God by themselves. These underground worship meetings of African Americans eventually surfaced as the public black church at the end of the Civil War (1865). It was on their own time and in their own spaces that blacks in chains re-created themselves with God.[1]

Memories of African Beliefs

White Christian slave traders and missionaries stole Africans from their homeland and disrupted their connections to the family of spirits and religious worldview of the African continent. Furthermore, these traders and missionaries forced speakers of different African languages to commingle, which weakened the memory of Africans as succeeding generations distanced themselves from their ancestral homelands and traditions. Yet enslaved Africans and African Americans retained some practices of African indigenous religions.[2]

In the worldview of those indigenous religions, the African High God ruled all creation with justice and compassion for the weak.[3] Getting their power from that supreme being, a group of intermediary gods carried out specific duties on behalf of the High God.[4] The ancestors, the living dead, were the most recent members of the spiritual world; they required, therefore, sacred acknowledgment and veneration. They too served an intermediary role, linking the plight and fortunes of the living with the supernatural realm.[5] Religious leaders and elders within the land of the living guided the community with sacred wisdom based on traditional authority. Finally, this worldview encompassed a vision of the unborn as preparing to depart from the spiritual to the material world.

African indigenous religions thus viewed the sacred and secular as one. Africans could not conceive of any space as nonreligious.[6] From the unborn state to the event of birth to the eventual return to the supernatural, all life was holy. This belief comforted and encouraged Africans. It comforted them because it suggested that God ruled over all creation and no individual or race could claim hegemony and monopoly in any sphere of reality. It encouraged them because whenever any person or group sought to challenge God's harmony by hoarding resources and lording privileges over another, duty called for ongoing resistance in the name of the supreme being.

In this scheme of things, individualism was a sin, but individuality was a cherished goal. In other words, in the African worldview, one left the human level and sank to a lower form whenever one acted to benefit primarily oneself. A human being could pursue her or his strengths and visions as long as they served the communal well-being. In radical distinction to certain European notions (e.g., "I think, therefore I am" — a notion that focuses on the self and opens the way toward a cutthroat competition for individual gain), Africans lived out an "I am because we are" style of life (a basis for a healthy collectivity that included the interests and needs of society's most marginalized).[7] Consequently, Africans lived in an extended family which not only biological kin but also the beggar, the broken, and the bereaved.

Finally, Africans brought with them to the "New World" a perspective that cherished "both-and," instead of "either-or." The High God ordained harmonious interaction and balance among human beings and between humanity and the natural and spiritual worlds. All of life's dimensions involved a complementary and nonantagonistic relationship with that which was outside of oneself. Thus the African perspective did not hold that a person or community which was different was naturally an enemy or an automatic threat. Only when evil spirits or wicked people disrupted the created balance of community did antagonisms and hierarchical stratification enter the picture.

Commonsense Wisdom

Hidden deep in the swamps and woods, with snakes and other wild animals as nature's witnesses, the Invisible Institution (which gave birth to the black church and was the soil for the roots of black theology) allowed enslaved African Americans to keep alive memories of African indigenous religions. To these, they added their own commonsense wisdom from everyday experience. These experiences consisted of sayings filled with folk theological wisdom. Most slaves knew, for example, what "God may not come when you call him, but he's right on time" meant. For them, the divinity was a time-God who operated on God's own time. From the human perspective, one could not control or always understand the ways of the All-Powerful. But — to paraphrase folk wisdom — somehow and some way, God appeared "on time" to ease your troubled mind, lift your burdens, prop you up on every leaning side, and help you climb the rough side of the mountain. It was this time-God who "made a way out of no way."

Similarly, the saying that "God sits high but looks low" provided an image of a majestic being whose providence covered all of reality. Though this All-Powerful One held the whole world in divine hands, still God knew the individual hairs on each of the heads of society's weak and downtrodden. Our arms might be too short to box with God (paraphrasing another slave saying), but this God was never positioned so high that the divine Spirit couldn't be bestowed on the human predicament. Indeed, the appearance of God's Word in the form of the human Jesus symbolized precisely the divine Being becoming poor in order to bring about suffering humanity's liberation. The revelation of Jesus is the death of the slave self and the resurrection of the new self. The divinity from above enters the poor's reality and brings a free life. Referencing the metaphor of being dead to sin/slavery and being resurrected to life/liberation, one former slave witnessed to his new Christian freedom brought to earth by the Spirit: "Whenever a man has been killed dead and made alive in Christ Jesus he no longer feels like he did when he was a servant of the devil. Sin kills dead but the spirit of God makes alive."[8]

The phrase "God don't like ugly" implied an absolute certainty that trouble did not last forever for the voiceless of society. Enslaved black Christians felt that though storm clouds might reign at the midnight hour, joy would come in the morning. Commenting on God's power in defeating slavery by bringing on the Civil War, ex-slave J. W. Lindsay proclaimed: "No res' fer niggers 'till God he step in an' put a stop to de white folks meanness."[9]

Perhaps evil might reign in the immediate realm, but in the end God's will would prevail on earth for the sufferers of pain and abuse. Such an expectation of the finality of justice gave the slaves hope in a future that would be theirs. Hope helped the poor to keep on struggling because God would take care of them through trials and tribulations. The ugliness of life had no dominion and would be defeated because the desire of the oppressed for full humanity coincided with God's dislike of evil.

The everyday experiences of the enslaved taught them that because God was on time, looked low, and detested ugliness, oppressed humanity was a co-laborer with God. We find this belief in another expression: "God helps those who help themselves." As sacred creations, human beings were compelled to defend themselves and struggle for full humanity in the course of achieving their fullest creative possibilities. For black chattel this meant a fight against the slave system. To wait idly on God while evil forces crushed down one's spirit, body, and mind meant a slow suicide. To the contrary, God called society's victims to co-labor with God and each other in life's dangerous vineyards in order to produce life's fullest fruit. This vision expressed the goal of ultimate freedom for the enslaved.

Reinterpretation of White Christianity

Enslaved African Americans took the preaching of white theology (which said, "Slaves, obey your masters"), transformed it, and used that transformed message as a plumb line which guided their understanding of the Bible and its implications for their unique situation. Whatever biblical stories spoke to the question of liberation and whatever events in their lives opened the door to freedom were used to guide their creative reevaluation of Christian talk about God. The intellectual brilliance of oppressed black workers and the burden of their status as private property (used for profit accumulation and as objects of pleasure for white folk) demanded a critical reinterpretation of the Bible. Liberation biblical stories were eagerly accepted and cherished as the criteria of Christian witness and evangelism. Likewise, liberation actions were lifted up as criteria for sensible biblical interpretation. The glue of justice for the poor held together both scriptural importance and daily practice.

From their perspective of freedom found in the memories about their African religious beliefs, in the commonsense wisdom of everyday experiences, and in the liberation theme at the heart of a reinterpreted Christianity, enslaved black workers projected themselves into an entirely new community made up of God, Jesus, their families, and themselves.

God became the main expression of justice. The European Christians and their descendants in North America had defined justice as saving the African "heathens" from the barbarism of their own native environment. But when enslaved Africans embraced the good news of the Bible, they sifted out the essence of true liberation. As one former slave wrote:

> Indeed I, with others, was often told by the minister how good God was in bringing us over to this country from dark and benighted Africa, and permitting us to listen to the sound of the gospel. To me, God also granted temporal freedom, which man without God's consent, had stolen away.[10]

This sense of freedom flowed directly from a slave interpretation of the Hebrew Scriptures. Here, in the lives of the Hebrew people, black workers saw a reflection of their own lives. Pharaoh occupied the role of the white slave masters. The story of oppression of the Israelites sounded exactly like black folk's experiences with southern and northern slavery in

America — it was a story of forced labor and a subordinate social status.

Consequently, if Yahweh could free those biblical people, then surely the same God (the I AM WHO I AM GOD) could and would liberate four million African Americans. In original creation, Yahweh had granted equal freedom to all humanity. But "man" (slave traders and profiteers in black flesh) had stolen the black people from Africa and thereby had betrayed God's sacred intent from the beginning of time. Just as the God of the Hebrew Scriptures brought new reality to oppressed Hebrews, so would the same God fulfill the promise of liberation for black workers in North American slavery.

Moreover, the enslaved developed a ritualistic affirmation about God's consistency. For them, God inevitably felt a special *love* for the oppressed, *heard* their groans, and *delivered* them out of the house of bondage. A former slave writes about the hell of North American slavery and the eventual decision of God to break the chains of captivity:

> The Lord, in His love for us and to us as a race, has ever found favor in His sight, for when we were in the land of bondage He heard the prayers of the faithful ones, and came to deliver them out of the Land of Egypt. For God loves those that are oppressed, and will save them when they cry unto him, and when they put their trust in Him.[11]

This ritual chant of sacred *love-hearing-deliverance* expressed the heart of the new liberation theology that slaves contributed to Christianity in North America. Neither the Massachusetts Pilgrims of 1620 nor the European colonialists who settled Jamestown, Virginia, in 1607 experienced so definitively a God who allowed the poor to "ever [find] favor in His sight." Now love included a divine partiality to the poor; hearing became Yahweh's ears opening to the moans of the voiceless of the earth; and deliverance saw the divinity with outstretched arms fighting off slavery and hoisting the victims on eagles' wings into a land rich with "milk and honey."

And this unfolding righteousness was all-inclusive. For instance, women chattel spoke of God as both male and female. After securing her freedom, an African American woman wrote that God "has been a father and a loving mother and all else to me."[12] This emphasis on the dual practical nature of God helped slave religion to develop a unique theology in the United States, one that spoke consistently to all victims of society.

Rereading the Bible

The second building block in the development of a black theology of liberation is a rereading of the Bible from the perspective of the majority of society, those who are poor and working people.

Black theology of liberation believes in a relationship between God's freeing activity in the African American community and that same liberating activity documented in the Hebrew and Christian Scriptures. In contrast to dominant ideas about theology, which claim to offer impartial thinking or talking about God, black theology sees and experiences the spirit of freedom clearly on the side of the African American poor. Biblical stories provide examples of God siding with oppressed people. And when they, the majority of the world, are able to practice spiritual and material freedom, then the minority groups who have a monopoly on most resources on earth will also have a chance to be free from their sin of keeping almost all of God's resources for themselves. Dominant theologies say they are universal. But they really wear a mask to hide the domination of the few over the many. Black theology of liberation states openly its leaning toward the majority of the world in order to work with the spirit of freedom for all.

At the foundation of the Hebrew Scriptures is a continuous

story about how Yahweh heard, saw, and delivered oppressed Hebrew slaves from bondage to liberation:

> I have observed the misery of my people who are in Egypt; I have heard their cry on account of their taskmasters. Indeed, I know their sufferings, and I have come down to deliver them from the Egyptians, and to bring them up out of that land to a good and broad land, a land flowing with milk and honey.... The cry of the Israelites has now come to me; I have also seen how the Egyptians oppress them. So come [Moses], I will send you to Pharaoh to bring my people, the Israelites, out of Egypt. (Exod. 3:6–11)

The biblical emancipation was not only freeing the invisible spirits of the slaves but also the freeing of real workers who were real slaves to the ruling class, whose purpose was the accumulation of profit based on the forced and unjust labor of working, oppressed humanity. The issue of poverty, therefore, stands at the heart of the Hebrew Scriptures. Poverty, as the result of injustice, cries out from the pages of the divinely inspired writings. Of all the classes, sectors, and strata in biblical times, Yahweh opted for the poor and decided consciously to listen to, to see, and to change the course of human history by cementing forever the holy will to a single purpose. This purpose was the freeing of broken humanity from sin by working with the poor on earth. Because Yahweh's being and work are liberation, Yahweh, out of divine love for the victims of oppression, set forth this divine purpose for humanity.

Similarly, the focal point of the Christian story is the decisive revelation of the God of liberation for the poor in Jesus of Nazareth. God so loved the world that God gave as a free gift the spirit of freedom in the body of Jesus (John 3:16). With Jesus, the Christian way toward full personal and communal liberation opens up for all of humanity. While Yahweh loved, heard, saw, and delivered a particular poor class and oppressed people, in the example of the Hebrews, the event of Jesus opens the divine promise of freedom for all of humanity who would give their way of life to the poor. Again, out of various options and possibilities, God (Yahweh) made a conscious decision to appear in a specific social location. The all-powerful God made up the divine mind, will, and feelings and chose a setting of poverty for the birth of the one chosen to offer full humanity for all. God intentionally disclosed God's self in the dirt and dung of a manger. Due to the lack of room for God at the inn, God appeared in squalor among the smell of farm animals.

Here in this divinely selected location of straw and manure, we see the continuation of the key thread of compassion for the poor related in the Hebrew Scriptures. In fact, the glue that holds together all of the stories of the Bible is God siding with the poor for everyone's full humanity on earth. No amount of spiritualizing or metaphysical discourse or methods of analogy can erase the clear biblical story of God in Jesus in the poverty of a manger. God revealed the divine self to humanity not by accident but with purpose and plan — that is, to give birth to the new humanity out of the surroundings of dirt, dung, and oppression. This is the first scandal of the Jesus story.

Moreover, from the words of Jesus (or in the memory of the tradition which followed him), we discover the continuation of this event of divinity and poverty in the first proclamation of Jesus the liberator. The divine Spirit in Jesus intentionally decided how to make the first public appearance of God's will known to all humanity. What would be the purpose and plan of God on earth? Who would God focus on to bring about a new heaven and a new earth? In the speech which began the entire ministry of Jesus, Jesus stated with power:

> The Spirit of the Lord is upon me, because It has anointed me to bring good news to the poor. It has sent me to proclaim release to the captives and recovery of sight to the blind, to let the oppressed go free, to proclaim the year of the Lord's favor. (Luke 4:18–19)

In the synagogue in Nazareth, Jesus chose intentionally the scroll of Isaiah 61 from the entire collection of Hebrew writings. And this crucial passage and inaugural proclamation revealed God's way for Jesus' ministry forever — the way of justice and righteousness for the poor. Again, no amount of spiritualizing of this passage can remove the divine emphasis on those in poverty and oppression. Those without wealth, those who are physically blind, those behind steel bars of real prisons, and those suffering material oppression are the recipients of God's good news. And what is this gospel message? The revelation of Jesus (e.g., Jesus' birth and opening statement clarifying the ways in which the divine will side with the poor) marks the fulfillment of the year of the Lord's favor, which was and is the freeing of real slaves and victims from many traps and tribulations.

Jesus not only establishes a clear, lifelong goal of liberation for all humanity at the beginning of his career but also gives us criteria for who will enter heaven and who will suffer for their earthly exploitation of the poor. He announces those criteria in Matt. 25:31ff., which is perhaps the only passage throughout the entire sixty-six books of the Bible where the criteria for entering heaven are exact.

Other passages about heaven and hell, such as those found in the book of Revelation, speak abstractly, and, as a result, one can talk about an abstract spirit and make up one's own vague symbols and images. This is what the dominant theology does. It uses abstract and vague language to hide its justification for a system of racism and oppression. In other words, it looks for general statements in the Bible so that it can make up its own subjective criteria for the arrival of the new community on earth as it is in heaven.

However, in Matt. 25:31ff., Jesus speaks plain words and gives God's criteria for salvation and liberation:

> When the Son of Man comes in his glory, and all the angels with him, then he will sit on the throne of his glory. All the

nations will be gathered before him and he will separate people one from another as a shepherd separates the sheep from the goats.

The division into sheep and goats, indicating who will enjoy the new earth and new heaven, clarifies the option that all of humanity has for liberation and salvation. Each person (e.g., rich and poor, white and black, male and female) has the ability to decide her or his response to divine grace or the gift of a fully free life. However, this liberation and salvation do not appear as a result of abstractions or invisible faiths. The full humanity for all people comes about according to their relation to those sectors of society who are materially poor:

> Come, you that are blessed by my Father, inherit the king-dom prepared for you from the foundation of the world; for I was hungry and you gave me food, I was thirsty and you gave me something to drink, I was a stranger and you welcomed me, I was naked and you gave me clothing, I was sick and you took care of me, I was in prison and you visited me.... Truly I tell you, just as you did it to one of the least of these who are members of my family, you did it to me. (Matt. 25:34–36, 40)

Here is the key for the full humanity of all peoples who opt for the poor. God is not a narrow divinity who arbitrarily sides exclusively with one people. God sides with the poor in order to present the universal divine grace (e.g., the opportunity) to all who have ears to hear and eyes to see the materially poor and oppressed: the hungry, the thirsty, the homeless strangers, the torn and tattered naked ones, the sick who lack resources or health insurance for their illnesses, and those in prisons, the majority of whom are overwhelmingly poor.

Black theology claims that the God of liberation witnessed to in the Bible, decisively revealed in the living presence of Jesus Christ, and offered today as an empowering Spirit is the same

God who desires the divine will to be located amidst the plight and struggle of the black poor. In the African American community, the vast majority fall into the category of workers and the poor, like the workers and the poor in the Hebrew and Christian Scriptures. Because God consciously gave the sacred will to live wherever the poor are, a black theology of liberation anchors itself in the interests of the black poor. This is where God lives and gives life. Because it is the divine will for the poor to be free (e.g., as revealed in the Hebrew and Christian Scriptures), the small, rich ruling classes of today have the opportunity to accept God's grace for them to choose for the poor. In fact, God's choice instructs the minority of every society to choose to share their monopolized wealth with the majority of the world. By returning God's resources to all of humanity, the minority group of monopolizers no longer will exploit the poor. Thus, by focusing on the poor, the exploiters and oppressors no longer are hurting the world's majority but are beginning to do God's will. Through the poor, the rich and all who monopolize receive their salvation.

Similarly, with the African American poor, we find the opportunity for all to make a conscious decision to attain their full humanity and enjoy the new social relations on earth and in heaven. The biblical revelation and the revelation of God among the black poor complement one another because they constitute the same holy event of liberation.

Developments in the 1950s and 1960s

In its process of development, black theology combined slave theology and a new reading of the Bible with black folk's affirmation of black pride and resistance against white racism during the momentous years of Martin Luther King Jr. and Malcolm X. More specifically, black theology as a twentieth-century Christian theology arose from three main endeavors:

(1) a critique of Joseph R. Washington Jr.'s *Black Religion;* (2) the civil rights movement of the 1950s and 1960s; and (3) the black power movement of the 1960s and early 1970s. The phrase "black theology" came out of the protest by and affirmation of black religion during this period of massive societal changes in the United States and in the Third World.

Black Religion

In 1964, Joseph R. Washington Jr., an African American religious scholar, published his *Black Religion.* In this text, Washington argued several points. First, he gave very specific definitions. Religion, for him, meant a belief in various dimensions of the human experience, but it was not the same thing as faith. Religion was only a partial reflection of faith. He wrote:

> Faith demands a fundamental change in the individual. Its direction is shaped and tested by a community of believers instructed by tradition and history. Faith must always be a response to God. Religion may be a response to whatever the individual desires. Faith stands in judgment on all religion, and is the critic of every religion. It is the concern with the Ultimate above every limited or limiting concern. Thus, faith is not concerned solely with one aspect of a man's life but with the whole of life. It is out of faith that one makes every decision and wills to be loyal to God in every moment. But in religion a man may place his value on some goal or god which he confuses with God.[13]

For example, religion could be a response to a political party or a justice movement or direct mass action. Faith, in contrast, meant a specific belief in God through Jesus Christ. "Faith begins with the cross and resurrection of Jesus Christ, not with the man from Nazareth or with the Sermon on the Mount. The Christian is one who has faith in Jesus Christ as Lord."[14] Consequently, faith could be found only in a tradition, especially the historic Protestant Christian tradition from Europe. Faith in Christ, grounded in the European tradition, could appear only in the institutional church. In other words, for Washington, the true church was one that has specific faith (as opposed to religion) in the God of the Hebrew and Christian Scriptures. Even a belief in the religion of Jesus did not stand as an authentic example of the true church. Furthermore, only with faith, tradition, and a church institution could one have and develop a theology. Theology, therefore, arises from a church grounded in a firm faith handed down through European tradition. For Washington, white Christians were true Christians because only they had *faith* in Christ, were connected to a white European Christian *tradition*, and belonged to the true *church* (as opposed to an organization). Therefore, white people were the only ones who had a Christian *theology*.

Second, Washington claimed that black people in the United States were religious and had developed religious institutions. This part of his analysis affirmed positively the historic struggle for justice, freedom, and equality of these religious institutions. For Washington, white churches could learn from this. In fact, Washington detected this affirmation of the struggle for justice for the least in society as far back as the slave church. If there was a problem regarding the history of contemporary black religious organizations, it was their deviation from their strong justice heritage throughout the decades after the slavery days.

However, Washington continued, a belief in the religion of justice or even a religion of the justice of Jesus did not qualify as faith. Faith can only be in God manifested in Jesus Christ, passed down from European Christian tradition, housed in European and white American churches today, and anchored in theology — an intellectual investigation of European and white American Christianity. As a result, he stated:

> Negroes have failed to make real contributions to Protestantism, the Christian faith, or the Christian Church,

or to suggest any ecclesiastical change in the white organizations after which they are modeled. The reason for
this failure is not inherent inability; it is primarily because
of the fact that Negro institutions were not established
to propound theology or liturgical matters.... [B]lack religion perverted the historic Christian faith.[15]

The key to Washington's analysis was his belief in the harmful impact of Christian white supremacy and the evils of segregation carried out by white Americans. Only white churches
had a faith (and not just religion) and were the heirs of European tradition. The sin of racism had forcefully kept black
people out of the Christian faith, tradition, church, and, consequently, theology: "The central theological questions of faith,
particularly the teachings of the Church on social issues, have
not entered the religious realm of the Negro."[16]

Therefore, if theology can arise only out of white churches,
which are the true defenders of the faith (as opposed to religion), then black religious organizations were at best institutions for justice and at worst mere organizations of childlike
clowning. The solution, for Washington, was for black religious
organizations to go out of business and join white American
churches in order to have access to theology. Once these black
religious organizations finally had access to (white) faith, their
positive contributions to white churches would be the emphasis
on and experience of justice work.

Many prominent white religious scholars and clergymen
hailed *Black Religion* because it was an intellectual statement
about the authenticity of white American churches and a bold
critique of the nature of the African American church. The book
was not merely an abstract academic treatise. On the contrary,
its publication arrived in the midst of the black church's leadership of the civil rights movement. Thus this book repositioned
the white church as the center of Christian faith and witness in
America. And its attack on black religion meant that African

American believers should give up their independent status and assimilate into white churches.

In contrast, though acknowledging Washington's under-scoring of the justice element of black believers, African American religious leaders condemned the book because of its uncompromising assertion that black religious worshipers did not have faith, were separated from Christian tradition, failed as churches, and thus lacked a theology. Washington's program asserted that if black people were to become a church and possess a theology, they would have to merge with whites and adopt a white theology. Black theologians were moved to show the shortsightedness of Washington's analysis. Consequently, black theology arose, in part, as a systematic investigation, development, and creation of a Christian theology for black people moving toward liberation.

The Civil Rights Movement

If Washington's academic publication proved a negative incentive for the emergence of a black theology of liberation, the civil rights and black power movements served as positive intellectual energy from the grassroots. The contemporary civil rights movement began on December 1, 1955.[17] On that day a black female worker, Rosa Parks, sat down in a Montgomery, Alabama, bus and refused to give her seat to a demanding white man. Her act of radical defiance against the evils of southern segregation laws sparked a new generation of black civil rights protest.

Because this black Christian woman was tired from a day's work and because she felt mistreated, Mrs. Parks began a movement that propelled Reverend Martin Luther King Jr., the African American church, and the North American black struggle for justice into the national and international arenas. For 382 days, King and the Montgomery black movement based in African American churches boycotted the city buses to protest segregation and walked for freedom. One old Christian black woman captured the determined spirit of protest. When asked about the weariness of walking to and from work, she replied: "My feets is tired, but my soul is rested."

It was these tired "feets" marching for freedom in the streets that symbolized the historic religious resistance of black Americans since slavery. Just as the secret slave church (the Invisible Institution) and the independent African Baptist and African Methodist churches had initiated and led the antebellum movement against the evils of slavery, the black church of the 1950s and 1960s, under King's leadership, played a vanguard role in breaking down legal segregation, primarily in the South. The African American church knew that the Christian gospel contradicted the discriminating laws of white supremacy. Meeting, organizing, worshiping, and singing in the church, the southern black community was empowered by the spirit of freedom.

The civil rights movement was a radical and militant chapter in the history of the African American struggle for liberation and the practice of freedom. It propelled the black church into direct mass action which broke laws. The movement emptied the pews of churches and enabled members to shut down the normal functions of local governments by disrupting the business-as-usual attitudes and practices of whites with power. Building on the persistent legal battles of the National Association for the Advancement of Colored People (NAACP) in the 1940s and early 1950s, the civil rights movement, through the African American church, brought in a new form of protest. Blacks moved from the court chambers dominated by the NAACP into the streets and backwoods of the southern states.

Massive boycotts, sit-ins, kneel-ins, and other acts of civil disobedience undermined Jim Crow practices and segregation laws. On the social level, the civil rights movement demanded full equality for all Americans within the rights of the U.S. Constitution. The religion of freedom, the historical religion of black faith from the time of slavery, fueled the movement against Ku Klux Klan terrorism, racist politicians, and a general white backlash.

Black theology arose from black pastors who had partic-ipated in King's civil rights movement. These ministers and church administrators were veterans of civil rights resistance in the South and desegregation battles in the North. They were familiar with water hoses and cattle prods. They had religiously told white officials to stick to Christian love and nonviolence. They had also preached funerals for nonviolent civil rights workers. And they experienced the pain of having their churches dynamited in the early morning hours.

The major lesson that the eventual founders of black theol-ogy of liberation took from the civil rights movement had to do with redefining what it meant to be church. That is to say, the movement redefined the church as a militant, radical man-ifestation of Jesus Christ in the streets on behalf of the poor and marginalized. The true African American church must wit-ness outside of buildings and on behalf of the least in society. The church had to follow the way of Jesus Christ, who came, died, and was resurrected for the freedom of the oppressed and, through them, of all humanity.

The Black Power Movement

The black power movement, the third incentive for the rise of a black theology of liberation, began with the call for black power during a civil rights march on June 16, 1966, in Green-wood, Mississippi. The march was headed by Dr. King and Stokely Carmichael, the chair of the Student Non-violent Co-ordinating Committee (SNCC — the youth wing of the civil rights movement). Because of the growing national and inter-national focus on southern efforts at justice at that time, Carmichael specifically chose this march to launch his slogan. Black power resistance therefore grew directly from the civil rights movement.

The movement did, however, have other roots. First, despite the 1954 Supreme Court decision that separate was not equal and despite white liberals' claims that the decade between 1955 and 1965 was one of Negro progress, the masses of black people suffered in every category concerning the standard of living. Between the successful 1955–56 Montgomery bus boycott and the signing of the Voting Rights Act in 1965, the gap between black and white in every sphere of American society had widened.[18] Despite the passage of the Civil Rights Acts of 1957, 1960, and 1964 and the Voting Rights Act of 1965, the decade of Negro progress referred to by whites applied to only a small sector of the black community. The African American middle class reaped meager benefits from the struggle for civil rights, but the black poor — the overwhelming majority — remained in poverty and lacked significant societal gains.

Second, increasing numbers of youth in the civil rights movement voiced a growing disdain toward the hypocrisy of white liberalism. The Student Non-violent Coordinating Committee reflected this changing mood. In opposition to the local, segregated Democratic Party, SNCC and Fannie Lou Hamer played a leading role in creating the Mississippi Freedom Democratic Party (MFDP) as a representative of the state's loyal (black) majority for the presidential ticket of Lyndon Johnson. However, at the 1964 Democratic National Convention in Atlantic City, Lyndon Johnson, Hubert Humphrey, Walter Mondale, and other white liberals on the convention's credentials committee, as well as black civil rights establishment leadership, supported the illegal white, segregationist, male delegation from Mississippi.

Suffering "betrayal at the hands of the white liberals," SNCC analyzed the defeat inflicted by the liberal-segregationist alliance at the 1964 Democratic Convention. By the convention's conclusion, the youth group "was convinced that membership in the Democratic coalition held little hope for Southern blacks and that, lacking power, they would always be sold out by the liberals."[19]

Third, in addition to the hypocrisy of liberal Democrats, the failure of federal government support for voter registration continued the disillusionment process for SNCC. In 1961 the Kennedy administration sought to redirect the growing militant energy of SNCC into voter registration in the Deep South. The president volunteered federal protection if the youth agreed to the proposed refocus. One wing of SNCC accepted the opportunity. But as early as the 1962 voter registration organizing, SNCC workers underwent bloody beatings from local segregationists as federal agents of Robert Kennedy's Justice Department stood nearby, watched, and took notes. Attorney General Robert Kennedy admitted that "careful explanations of the historic limitations on the federal government's police powers [were] not satisfactory to the parents of students who have vanished in Mississippi."[20]

Fourth, black power arose in reaction to white segregationist terrorism in the South. The stakes for registering to vote proved to be deadly. SNCC activists and local black residents experienced bombings, beatings, shootings, burnings, maiming, kidnaping, sabotaging of cars, and murder. Along with this vigilante violence, the system used various "legal" means of repression: sheriffs jailed "outside agitators" who disrupted the normal ties between whites and blacks; banks and insurance companies conveniently canceled loans and policies, thereby intimidating powerless black sharecroppers and farmworkers; and politicians, from state governors down to city council members, simply ignored federal mandates by upholding the doctrine of "interposition and nullification" (states' rights).

Finally, black power (proclaimed in June 1966) revealed the resurrection of the spirit of Malcolm X (assassinated in February 1965), the contemporary father of black nationalism. More than any other public figure in the late 1950s and early 1960s, Malcolm grasped the profound sense of psychological self-hatred and self-denigration internalized by black America.

With biting, insightful clarity he declared, "The worst crime the white man has committed has been to teach us to hate ourselves."[21] That is why black people burned their hair to make it straight. And for similar reasons, they bleached their skin and tried to make their noses and lips thinner. In addition to denying their natural and beautiful self-identity by burning their hair and distorting their skin (thus rejecting the gifts with which God had blessed them), African Americans did not share equitably in the resources of the nation. White men controlled the major institutional resources of America. To love oneself, then, meant both the right of self-identity (e.g., black is beautiful) and the right of self-determination (e.g., the control of the means of producing and distributing the nation's wealth).

Furthermore, Malcolm explained the true meaning of integration — white communities coming together in white ethnic groups and using power while calling on blacks to appeal to the moral consciousness of the dominant society. Malcolm sought to shatter the myth in the black person's mind that equated value and all positive norms with whiteness and that also defined blackness as a creation of whites. Before black power, white people stood for cleanliness, beauty, and saintliness. Black people were equal to nastiness, ugliness, and evil.

Like a tireless Hebrew Scripture prophet wielding the flaming sword of truth against "principalities and powers," Malcolm X demanded black liberation "by any means necessary." Politically, he preached black solidarity and the right of self-determination. Culturally, he lifted up black pride and Pan-Africanism. And theologically, he defined the white man as "the devil."

In the midst of the 1966 cry for black power, urban rebellions, and political and cultural demands in the African American community, black theology was born. African American pastors, church administrators, and laypersons found themselves at a crossroads. On the one hand, many of them had been staunch participants in the civil rights movement. On the other, the radical shift of the freedom movement to black power and the involvement of many of their own community in this new event presented a dilemma. African American Christians found themselves stuck with a theology that was suitable for the "We Shall Overcome" religion of integration and white liberals but that was apparently insufficient and irrelevant to the needs of the African American community which was shouting "I'm black and I'm proud!"

In the hurricane eye of a black revolution, the ad hoc National Committee of Negro Churchmen (NCNC) formed to reply to the new black power initiative.[22] As noted above, they chose to publish a full-page black power statement in the July 31, 1966, edition of the *New York Times*. The statement presented a favorable theological interpretation of black power. Basing their thought in the black power movement, the originators of a black theology of liberation concluded that theology (i.e., faith in and witness with a God of freedom) had something to do with power. The history of black and white Americans had always been a system of unequal social relations. White Christians monopolized power without conscience while blacks had conscience but no power.

In the fall of 1968, Gayraud S. Wilmore, an early chairperson of the NCNC theological commission, described "the rising crescendo of voices from the pulpit and pew demanding that black churchmen reexamine their beliefs; that unless they begin to speak and act relevantly in the present crisis they must prepare to die." The black protest movement presented an ultimatum: unless African American pastors " 'do their thing' in some kind of symbolic and actual disengagement from the opprobrium of a white racist Christianity, they have no right to exist in the black community."[23]

The voices and protest of black people forced the issue of the role of Christianity in the African American community. Thus black theology arose to affirm African American humanity and as an answer to the reality of black liberation moving against white racism. Where was God and Jesus Christ in the urban areas of rebellions? Was the African American church simply serving an "Uncle Tom," otherworldly role, or was it aiding in black control of the community and black people's destiny? Could African Americans continue to uphold the theology of integration and liberalism? When stripped of its "whiteness," what did Christianity say to black Americans? Could black identity, culture, history, and language become authentic sources for developing theology? If not, could one be black and Christian? Furthermore, in the expanding African American revolt, what did a blue-eyed, blond-haired, "hippie-looking" Jesus have to do with black power and black liberation?

By 1966 a growing number of African American ministers who had faithfully followed King found themselves at a crossroads between King's nonviolent Christian philosophy, on the one hand, and black power, urban rebellions, and Malcolm X's black nationalist philosophy, on the other. Thus black theology came from a mixture of King's Christian gospel of racial justice and black power's black liberation nationalism. African American religious leaders began to conclude that the God of Moses and Jesus did not support slavery and segregation. Quite the opposite, authentic Christianity meant racial justice and black liberation by any means necessary.[24]

For example, one of the creators of the National Committee of Negro Churchmen has stated that the committee was formed when a group of black churchpeople "found ourselves in a vacuum." The turbulence in the African American community had caused more and more black churchpeople to choose between the "vacuum" of integrationism and the relevancy of black liberation. He continued: "We had gotten to the point where we had to hear God speaking through what we [the African American church and community] were going through."[25] And where did the committee hear the word of God? Previously the white church power-structure had supported and given money to only the formally educated and "reasonable" Negro church leaders such as Martin Luther King Jr. No matter how many marches civil rights churches and organizations led against racism, the white church suspected that it shared the same "theology" with the black church. The white church could draw on a common theological framework and speak a common theological language.

In complete contradiction to this integrationist, white liberal theological scheme, NCNC began to hear the word of God elsewhere. Another early figure in NCNC remembers how the committee

> began to talk about what would be the response of the black church, not simply to what Martin Luther King Jr. was doing, because many people were participating in [the civil rights movement] as churches, but also to take some account of the more militant groups such as the Black Muslims,...Black Panthers, Ron Karenga's group, ...[and] Stokely Carmichael.[26]

Although the seeds of black theology in the United States first sprouted with the formation of the NCNC in 1966 (the group later decided to change its sexist name to the National Conference of Black Churches), it was not until the spring of 1969 that these early attempts at new life bore their first fruit. James H. Cone's *Black Theology and Black Power* appeared in March 1969.[27] The NCNC and the African American church finally had a scholarly work which sharply presented the black religious experience not merely as a challenge to the practice of the white church but also as a devastating criticism of the faith existing in both white and African American churches. Cone argued, in brief, that black power was the gospel of Jesus Christ.

Cone's unique emphasis is introducing liberation of the poor, specifically the African American poor, as the key to all types of theology and church practice. The heart of the gospel of Jesus Christ is the liberation of the oppressed who live as victims due to systems of evil. For Cone, in fact, Jesus Christ himself is the liberator of the oppressed. Because Jesus is for the oppressed and because African Americans are oppressed, Jesus must be the black Christ who provides the necessary soul for black liberation. Moreover, the church must be with the poor because Jesus is already there suffering with them in their pain and struggling with them for their full humanity.

Method of Black Theology

In addition to the radical Christian religion created by enslaved African Americans (i.e., God's revelation in slavery), a new reading of the Bible (i.e., God's revelation in a sacred book), and the civil rights and black power movements (i.e., God's revelation in recent history), the fourth and final building block in the development of black theology as a theology of liberation is method (i.e., God's revelation today and in the future). Method helps the African American church to carry out the content of black theology. And this content is God's spirit of liberation located among the poor, whose freedom has implications for the full humanity of all. For the Christian, the decisive revelation of this divine content is Jesus Christ.

Furthermore, method in theology responds to the question: How do we arrive at our answers in our talk about and practice with God among the poor today? How do we come to our conclusions about relations among God, humanity, and the world? What sources are our starting point? What are our key beliefs? What norm helps us to distinguish between sinful spirits and the divine liberation spirit? What are the consequences of our theology? For today and the future, method helps the black church and other communities organizing for justice to find out where to work in order to be with God, who is already with the African American poor.

Sources

Black theology of liberation is a systematic and constructive movement arising from the reality of God's liberation power existing in all parts of life. There is no separation of sacred and secular because God's love for the least of society has no boundaries. The spirit of God's liberation is present in all aspects of black existence, especially that of the poor. In black theology, sources answer the question about the location of the meeting between divine revelation and black humanity. Where do the African American poor meet God's presence and action for liberation? Where and how does God's spirit of liberation reveal itself? There are at least six important sources in black theology of liberation.

The first source of black theology is the Bible. Today's poor African Americans struggle for freedom and encounter oppressed conditions similar to those in the Hebrew and Christian Scriptures. The Hebrew Scriptures reveal Yahweh compassionately hearing and seeing the dire difficulties experienced by the least in society, in this case, the Hebrew slaves. When the poor today read the story of Hebrew slaves and their relationship to a liberator God, they can see that they are not alone in their cruel predicament in contemporary America.

The biblical stories of exodus feature an oppressed people (i.e., the Hebrews) who suffered at the hands of brutal taskmasters; were accused falsely; were pursued by forces of prejudice; dwelled in the midst of a wilderness experience; went through periods of anxiety, fear, and doubt about the future, at times longing for a return to their former status in an inhuman system; and quarreled with their leaders while doggedly continuing along the way to freedom. Each element of this story has a deep resonance for African Americans.

Moreover, the African American poor, reading the Hebrew Scriptures from their position on the bottom of American society, discover a whole new world different from the dominating

Christianity and theology of mainstream American believers. The exodus theme does not end with harsh difficulties. On the contrary, the hope of deliverance cancels out the pain and gives today's poor the strength to "keep on keeping on." The certainty of victory, witnessed to in the Hebrew Scriptures, gives the poor strength in the midst of their deepest self-doubt caused by seemingly insurmountable odds.

Likewise, the black poor bring their own contextual concerns to the Christian Scriptures. And Jesus meets and greets them as their liberator, as the one who can perform miracles — turning "the impossible into the possible." The lowly birth of Jesus; his singular purpose to be with, struggle with, and set free the oppressed; his constant harassment by official authorities who questioned his claims to usher in a new Common Wealth for the least in his day; his eventual death applauded by government officials and the police; and his final triumph by way of rising out of the clutches of evil — all these bring good news of possibilities and power for the poor. Thus the first source of black theology is the unity between, on the one hand, the pain and promise of oppression and liberation found in the Bible and, on the other hand, a similar existence experienced by the African American poor people today.

Black theology's second source is the African American church. The black church exists wherever black Christians come together in their own space and time to worship and live out God's call for freedom for the least in society. In this sense, the black church is the historical black churches (e.g., Baptist, African Methodist Episcopal, African Methodist Episcopal Zion, and Christian Methodist Episcopal), newer black churches (e.g., Pentecostal, Holiness, and nondenominational), and black church congregations in white denominations.

The African American church still is the most organized institution controlled solely by black people. It is predominantly made up of poor and working people, of which at least 70 percent are women. Its class and gender composition provides a fertile basis for the development, construction, and implementation of a black theology of liberation because African American women are usually at the bottom of American society and the black church is usually located in the heart of the black community.

Also, the black church's vibrant worship experiences, filled with holiness, help its members to direct their spiritual and emotional strength into forms of self-respect and "somebodyness," vital ingredients for long-term struggle. Its language and rhythm of preaching, praying, singing, shouting, dancing, and testifying empower the cultural aspects of African American life, thus confirming that black English, call-and-response styles (e.g., when the pastor preaches and the congregation starts to talk back), and sacred movements of the body are worthy and authentic. Its economic resources and other forms of wealth (e.g., buildings, publishing houses, transportation vehicles, auditoriums, dining facilities, credit unions) on a national scale could offer an independent financial base of alternative independent witnessing in a society continually making black life and labor unimportant and expendable.

The third source of black theology is a faith tradition of struggle for liberation. The African American church has a strong history of preaching and practice for justice — starting from the indigenous African religions of the first Africans forced to the "New World," through the secret Invisible Institution of slave religion, until today, when liberating Christianity is situated in some African American churches on the local level. At the same time, a faith tradition of struggle has existed outside formal church structures, most notably during the various periods of justice work by black civic, cultural, student, women's, and political organizations. God has offered the spirit of freedom wherever God has chosen to freely give freedom.

African American women's experience makes up the fourth source. If black women make up at least 70 percent of black churches and over half of the African American community, then black theology must deal with and reflect the intellectual, emotional, and body concerns and contributions of black women. There will never be a complete and real expression of black theology if African American women are absent. It would be a contradiction for black theology to link itself to liberation struggles yet voice only the minority male issues within its community.

The fifth source of black theology is culture — art, literature, music, folktales, black English, and rhythm. Liberation motifs in nonexplicit Christian texts have always been with African Americans. For example, the heroic and courageous stories about Anansi the Spider — a small, weak creature able to outsmart those with power — were brought by slaves from the west coast of Africa to American slave colonies and were passed orally from one generation to another. Jazz too served periodically as a creative and unique form of protest, refusing to fit within prescribed styles and themes of European- and Euro-American-controlled music. Black people's specific approach to sports, which takes place when black athletes celebrate with their in-your-face flair, is a unique way of declaring "I am somebody" in a world controlled by others of a different class and color. The extended family, another art form, has provided a way of survival and maintenance, but also a site for grooming and affirming the minds of the young who could possibly one day become the Harriet Tubmans, Sojourner Truths, Martin Kings, and Malcolm Xs of the future. A liberating culture is vital for a constructive black theology.

The sixth source is a radical politics. Here politics is the ability to determine the direction that the African American community can pursue. It is the right of self-determination. In order to achieve this type of freedom or full humanity, politics takes into account the vital importance of owning and controlling capital and resources. The key issue is making sure black poor people own and control the wealth. Wealth is different from income. Income is what working-class people receive from others who own and control wealth. To understand how capital and resources relate to the political direction of the African American community, we need a social analysis that will help poor black folk see the connection between global monopoly capital and its control of the U.S. domestic economy. Likewise, a helpful social analysis will aid in creating a concrete vision of a completely new future society based not on profit but on the well-being of all the poor in America.

The Norm in Black Theology

Yet what is it that flows throughout any source of black theology which makes black theology a form of God-talk and God-walk dealing with libertion? It is the presence of the spirit of liberation, a spirit that permeates, vivifies, and judges the usefulness of each source. In other words, the key to all talk about God from the perspective of the black poor is the spirit of liberation. Not all sources, histories, and contemporary experiences of African American people are locations of God's spirit of liberation for the poor. Some spirits are demonic: they support the status quo and keep poor black folk at the bottom while allowing a few African American middle-class people to "succeed." The African American experience, including that of the poor, is not automatically for liberation and full humanity. However, the black poor are the most fertile ground for the appearance of divine presence because it is God's will that they be free spiritually and materially. Moreover, the poor have no private ownership or no monopolization of capital or wealth in this world. Therefore, they have nothing to lose in the movement to bring about, with God, a new Common Wealth on earth as it is in heaven. But this "most fertile ground" can achieve its full potential only if the poor are practicing justice for the majority of society. Again, God's spirit of liberation (the spirit of freedom, justice, and the move toward full humanity) represents the norm.

Rhythm

Method not only is made up of sources and a norm but also includes the rhythm of doing theology. The rhythm of black theology starts from faith in, commitment to, worship with, and work for the poor in the African American community. This is the first part of the rhythm. Because the spirit of comfort, hope, and liberation exists among the least in society even before the theologian works with them, the theologian has to be connected to this dynamic between the poor and a liberation spirituality.

From a relationship with the poor and their concerns, theology follows as a second step within the rhythm of black theology. In fact, theology is self-critical thinking about the practice and faith of liberation of grassroots people within the church and the nonchurch.

The third dimension of black theology's methodological rhythm is the return of theology to the practice of faith to further the pastoral, ethical, political, cultural, economic, linguistic, and everyday way of life of the African American poor trying "to make a way out of no way" with their liberator God. And the rhythm continues. We start with the practice of faith, move toward thinking about theology, and return to the practice of faith. Key at each moment is whether or not the spirit of freedom is present.

Moreover, each of the three beats of the rhythm requires interpretation consisting of context, content, construction, and commitment. What is the *context* of the community of faith involved in struggle on a daily basis? What are the structural, the routine, the cultural, and the language parts of that community? The poor are born into a given multilayered context. What is the *content* of this contextual framework? The context is filled with content — creative resources and new experiences at the service of the poor. What type of constructive activities are taking place? In other words, how has God called the poor to use this context and content to build something new?

The poor's vocational act is the connection between context and content, thereby creating some type of different reality — a new *construction*. What unifies each step is the personal and collective *commitment* to the liberation of the poor. Do the context, content, and construction constitute commitments that are liberational or harmful? Black theology of liberation, then, is God's love for the least in society, and this love works to bring about each person's full humanity.

Black theology of liberation is an ongoing movement of God's Spirit of liberation in the Bible, revealed decisively in the living presence of Jesus, and manifested in the African American experience in solidarity with all of the poor. It is made up of people who are self-critical while they work with God to bring about liberation for all of humanity and the entire creation. And it is a vocation, a calling, from a spirit greater than oneself to maintain the church, the community, the family, and oneself on the path toward the practice of freedom.

Chapter 2

The First Generation

The four building blocks for the foundation of a black theology of liberation were accepted as crucial starting points by the founders of contemporary black theology. In other words, the first generation of African American religious scholars and pastors drew on slave religion, a reinterpretation of the Bible, the broad political and cultural currents within the civil rights and black power movements, and the new method of doing theology. Given these building blocks, the first generation — who were mainly male clergy and professors — then began to focus on the various aspects of actually constructing a black theology of liberation.

This first period stretched from 1966 (when the National Committee of Negro Churchmen published their black power statement in the *New York Times*) to the mid-1980s (when black women developed womanist theology and the second generation of black theologians began to emerge). It was a very vibrant time in American society and the entire world, especially in the Third World areas which were controlled by European colonialism.

In the United States, the civil rights and black power movements were struggling to lead the African American community and other poor people into the mainstream of American society and to establish the right of black communities to control their own political and economic resources and to define their own cultural identity. Throughout the 1960s to the early 1980s, black people began to assert their political rights by

electing African American mayors and state and federal representatives. They also attempted to implement the right of
self-determination in the economic arena with plans for community control. They did this by promoting self-help programs
and by demanding that the federal government invest in the
economic development of the inner cities.

During these years, the key issue for the political leaders
was that a small group of white males controlled the nation's
resources while excluding the overwhelming majority of American citizens. These black leaders saw American democracy as
simply a cover for white males' monopoly of power. In other
words, American democracy was an exclusive society where a
certain group occupied most of the elected offices, and this same
group of people dominated the major businesses and industries
in the country and throughout most of the world.

The goal of political self-determination was closely linked to
the fight for black self-identity. Was it possible to be black and
American? Or could a black person become fully human and
American only by becoming a carbon copy of white people?
Activists and leaders during the 1960s through the early 1980s
called on the African American community to love their own
black selves — skin color, hair texture, art, music, black English,
dance, poetry, philosophy, clothes, African names, black rituals
and holidays, history, heroes and heroines, connections to the
African continent, and celebration of their ancestors who were
enslaved in the democracy of the New World. In other words,
the right of cultural self-identity basically meant to love one's
black self first in order to love someone else.

The first generation of black theologians were greatly affected by this development in the broader society. As a result,
they began to raise questions about the Christian understanding of love and the relationship between blackness and being
created in the image of God. Why did American churches always paint God and Jesus as white men when God was a spirit
and the only white people in the Bible were the Roman colo-

nialists? African Americans were asserting black as beautiful, and African American clergy and professors began to listen.

Black theologians and movements in the larger black communities were, in addition, in conversation with and learning from groups in the Third World who were fighting against European and U.S. colonialism and for national liberation. European and U.S. colonialism, as one form of imperialism, was a natural outgrowth of capitalism and its need to make ever-increasing profits, a process that demanded wresting control of countries from those who inhabited them. Third World national liberation movements in Africa, particularly southern Africa, in Southeast Asia, particularly Vietnam, and in Latin America were organizing for political control of their own countries. They were opposed to a monopoly capitalist democracy and wanted to set up their own type of political systems with their own kinds of election processes. Moreover, they had to fight to control the wealth of their countries because European and American monopoly capitalists owned or controlled the global distribution of the natural resources in Third World nations.

Another important political development affecting the rise of the first generation of black theologians was the effort to create a Pan-Africanist coalition of people of African descent who lived throughout the world. Not only did first-generation clergy and professors participate in political meetings in Africa; they also attended conferences on Third World liberation theology. For example, the Ecumenical Association of Third World Theologians was started by an African student, and the first meeting of the group was held in Africa (1976).

Connected with this global desire of the people of the Third World for political self-determination was their goal of the right of self-identity, that is, the right to be human beings without imitating European and American culture. During this time, the Negritude movement in certain African countries was a prime example of the attempt to develop a unique African or black culture which drew on African beauty, philosophy, language, worldview, music, poetry, art, sculpture, plays, and so on.[1]

Similarly, the black consciousness movement in South Africa, headed by Steve Biko, had a strong program against black self-hatred and for love of the beautiful black self. Black consciousness, Biko wrote in 1971, "is a manifestation of a new realisation that by seeking to run away from themselves and to emulate the white man, blacks are insulting the intelligence of whoever created them black." Here Biko suggests that no black person could imitate white values, language, and culture and then claim that he or she was created by God. Either whites created blacks, or the Creator made black life. Biko continued: "Black Consciousness...takes cognizance of the deliberateness of God's plan in creating black people black."[2]

In the midst of these rapid changes in North American and global social relations, the first generation of black theologians began to create two main trends or two different approaches in their faith and practice — the political and the cultural. The rest of this chapter discusses representatives of each of these trends.

Advocating a Faith Revealed in Politics

African American political theologians give weight to opposing racism in the white American political system, church, and theology. As a group they respond to the 1966 black power call for African Americans to fight inhuman practices of white political power. They expose white Americans' use of religion and theology to justify any maintenance of white rule over black life. For the political theologians, black theology has to serve African American people's daily struggle against the grip of a white power-structure. They want to know how theology and the church aid in eliminating poor education, right-wing terror, police brutality, insensitive and corrupt politicians, the hopeless job situation of black youth, rat-infested ghettoes, the lack of

civil and human rights, and all situations in which whites control African American humanity. To combat white supremacist
power, the political theology group chooses theology (e.g., what
the black church says about and does with God) as its area of
resistance.

Each theologian in the political trend acknowledges the contribution of his colleagues. But, at the same time, each builds on
the existing state of black theology by contributing something
new to the overall political theological trend. Put differently,
within the political trend, the theologians complement and contrast with one another as they struggle together against the
main enemy — the racist politics of white theology. This means
that they confront the racism in white theology, and they use
theology to confront the white supremacist power-structure in
the broader society. The political theologians believe that it is
a God-ordained gift for African American people to fight to
change the unjust and inhuman power-relations in American
society. And they want to discover how black theology can be
involved in that movement.

In this first section we look at two representatives of the
black political trend — James H. Cone and J. Deotis Roberts.
The theological categories of (1) black theology, (2) liberation,
(3) christology, and (4) reconciliation will help us to examine each theologian's viewpoint on black theology and political
power-relations.

James H. Cone

Black Theology. James H. Cone is a distinguished professor
of systematic theology at Union Theological Seminary, New
York City, and a member of the Society for the Study of
Black Religion and the Ecumenical Association of Third World
Theologians. His black theology developed in response to the
civil rights and black power movements and northern urban
rebellions of the 1960s. Cone began his black theology by inter-

preting the black liberation movement through the systematic doctrines of classical theology. In this sense, Cone remained in the mainstream of classical theology.[3]

Among the political theologians, Cone's unique emphasis is introducing liberation of the poor, specifically the black poor, as the controlling key or norm of a political black theology. Cone wrote his first text during the upheaval of 1968. A white assassin's bullet had ended the life of Martin Luther King Jr. in April of that year. With that bullet the movement for peace, nonviolence, and racial fellowship ground to a halt. Within a week of King's murder, 130 U.S. cities went up in flames. The national guard and army troops descended upon the black ghettoes. Forty-six civilians died; over three thousand were injured; and twenty-seven thousand were arrested. Whites with structural power had intensified their war on black America.

Prior to 1968, however, and throughout his graduate studies and early teaching career, Cone knew of the increased attacks on the African American community. During 1967, while teaching at Adrian College in Adrian, Michigan, seventy miles from Detroit, he was deeply affected by the Detroit rebellion. Moreover, he read about the loss of black life at the hands of callous systemic white power. Between 1965 and 1968, three hundred urban riots erupted with over eight thousand casualties and fifty thousand arrested. Furthermore, Cone sensed the racist, white backlash which resulted in the 1968 presidential election of Richard M. Nixon. Nixon campaigned and won on a law-and-order platform. He pledged to fight against the civil rights gains of the 1960s. He decreased open housing, halted busing for school desegregation, reduced government funding for ghetto improvement, removed curbs on police departments, and gutted affirmative action policies. During 1968, Nixon and FBI director J. Edgar Hoover intensified counterintelligence programs to disrupt black protest organizations and assassinate black militants. While African Americans died, the overwhelming majority of white scholars engaged in intellectual conversations which were unrelated to God and the survival and freedom of black humanity.[4]

For Cone in 1968, therefore, the life of his community and his own black identity were at stake. He had to write on black theology and black power. If Christianity were to have any meaning for powerless black America, Cone wrote, it must reveal that the liberation of the black poor is at the core of the gospel. Thus Cone formulated his black theology in direct relation to the black power movement and urban rebellions in the 1960s. In 1970, he wrote:

> Black Power and Black theology work on two separate but similar fronts. Both believe Blackness is the primary datum of human experience which must be reckoned with, for it is the reason for our oppression and the only tool for our liberation.[5]

Cone (an African Methodist Episcopal clergy person) advocated a black theology that sought power for oppressed black people, a power that would be used to eliminate racist oppression and to enhance African American freedom. Similar to Malcolm X's faith claim, Cone called for a religion whose theological cornerstone was the demand for the political eradication of racial discrimination. Reviewing the birth of his black theology eighteen years later, he said: "I think when I first began [writing black theology], I saw the political as the most crucial. I still, in many ways, do." However, he wishes to "balance" the political-cultural dynamic "a lot more." Now he more tightly interweaves his understanding of these two strands: "I see the political and the cultural now with the political really dependent upon the cultural. I don't see how you can sustain a political analysis and movement without cultural resources."[6]

Here too, we can see his leaning toward the black political trend. Though hindsight has informed his theological combination of the political with the cultural, Cone has remained committed to a black theology that uses cultural resources *for* the political movement, the political liberation of black people.

I interpret the theological writings of Cone, the major representative of the black political theology trend of the first generation, as a black Christian theology of liberation.

Liberation. What does the gospel of liberation mean in Cone's theological system? The target of liberation for Cone is the destruction of the structure of American white racism. This demonic system has crushed the black person into a nonperson. "The white structure of this American society," Cone elaborates, "personified in every racist, must be at least part of what the New Testament meant by the demonic forces."[7] Though he later broadens the target to include women's oppression, capitalism, and imperialism, his entry point in the development of his black theology is African American people's struggle against racism.

For Cone, the movement toward black liberation and against this demonic structure begins in divine freedom. The freedom of God "is the source and content of human freedom." Divine freedom (meaning God's choice to create humans in freedom and to be with them in the realization of freedom and liberation in history) is thus the basis of black liberation or black freedom. The *image of God* (which is part of all people) determines humanity's created state and long-term goal in life. The original creation and the final goal are one: liberation and full humanity. At the same time, we cannot have divine freedom — and human freedom — without divine justice. Freedom or liberation goes along with justice. And divine justice makes black liberation more than a human effort and goal; it makes liberation a divine movement. God's righteousness and God's freedom help to bring about the liberation of humanity in history.[8]

In addition to holding together the concepts of divine freedom and divine justice/righteousness, liberation also links up with salvation and with "God's kingdom" in Cone's theology. Salvation is no longer a passive inward calmness or invisible cure in the afterworld; thus it no longer acts like a harmful drug in support of racism. On the contrary, God, through Christ, saves humanity by entering the depths of pain and oppression and liberating humanity from all human evils, including racism.

Finally, Cone sounds a universal note of liberation in his doctrine of the kingdom. The kingdom stands for all the world's poor because they have nothing to expect from this world. The kingdom will be freedom for all the oppressed in human history. The kingdom stands for the poor's hope and empowers them toward organizing for practical liberation in history.[9]

Christology. God's liberation of African American people through Christ's cross and resurrection pinpoints the core of Cone's christology (i.e., the identity and work of Jesus Christ). For Cone, the New Testament witness reveals Jesus' person as the oppressed one. Because black people suffocate under extreme difficulties, the center of Jesus' work is a black Christ identified with liberation from black suffering. The Bible tells the story of Jesus' oppression; the contemporary story tells of African American people's oppression. In a word, Jesus' identity as the oppressed one who takes on black suffering expresses the essence of divine identity and divine activity. Christ is black because of how Christ was revealed and because of where Christ seeks to be (i.e., with the African American poor). Having joined the liberation of the oppressed with the identity and work of Christ and having situated that liberation in the black community, Cone asserts boldly in his first published book, "Christianity is not alien to Black Power; it is Black Power."[10]

These emphases of Cone's lead him to oppose J. Deotis Roberts's contention that African Americans need a black Christ because of a psychocultural crisis.[11] Cone cites a distinction between the literal and symbolic nature of christological blackness. In explaining the contrast, Cone offers a warning regarding a black christology. "I realize," he confesses, "that 'blackness' as a christological title may not be appropriate in the distant future or even in every human context in our present." But today the literalness of Christ's blackness arises from Christ's entering and converging literally with black oppression and black struggle. Furthermore, Cone continues, Christ's symbolic status of blackness appears in Christ's "transcendent affirmation" that God has never left the universal oppressed alone.[12] A black Christ affirms the freedom of all the poor.

Cone's political doctrine of Jesus adds a new dimension. In order to fight white theology, Cone brings together both the Jesus of history and the Christ of faith to complement the liberation theme; we cannot have one without the other. He does argue that we know what and where Jesus is today based on what Jesus did while on earth. But at the same time, Cone creates new political meaning in the crucifixion and resurrection around the theme of liberation. Calvary (i.e., the crucifixion) and the empty tomb (i.e., the resurrection) prove key in Cone's christology. Jesus' "death and resurrection" reveal "that God is present in all dimensions of human liberation."[13]

Finally, Cone's black christology focuses on the poor. Christ died on the cross and rose from the dead to liberate the poor and the oppressed in direct opposition to the spirit of evil on earth. The identity and work of Christ express the divine intent to liberate the oppressed. Christ rescues the downtrodden from the material bondage of "principalities and powers." In this liberation process the oppressors also gain their freedom because the object of their oppression — the now-freed poor — no longer occupies an oppressed status.[14] The dynamic effect of Jesus Christ bringing deliverance for both the oppressed and the oppressor raises the question of the importance of reconciliation in Cone's black theology.

Reconciliation. Even though his first book (*Black Theology and Black Power,* 1969) is a thundering manifesto against white people and their racism, Cone never excludes the possibility of reconciliation:

I do not rule out the possibility of creative changes, even in
the lives of oppressors. It is illegitimate to sit in judgment
on another man, deciding how he will or must respond.
That is another form of oppression.[15]

The white oppressor might change and become reconciled with
the black oppressed in the latter's liberation movement. Here,
too, Cone differentiates his doctrine of reconciliation from that
of J. Deotis Roberts. Roberts believes that the essence of the
Bible dictates that blacks should reconcile with whites. For
Cone, the essence of the gospel calls first not for relations with
whites but for the practice of freedom for the black poor.

Cone develops his doctrine of reconciliation primarily and
consistently with concern for the liberation of oppressed African Americans. Therefore, in order to bring about meaningful
and productive reconciliation, only the black community can set
the conditions for reconciliation. The "white oppressor" suf-
fers from an enslavement to racism and cannot provide the
rules for real reconciliation. The oppressed are the ones who
must lay down "the rules of the game." The rule established by
oppressed African Americans aims at the heart of white racist
power. In fact, Cone writes, "there will be no more talk about
reconciliation until a redistribution of power has taken place.
And until then, it would be advisable for whites to leave blacks
alone."[16]

Cone describes two types of reconciliation — objective and
subjective. Because Jesus Christ died on the cross and rose from
the dead, the devil and satanic forces experienced defeat. This
cross-resurrection triumph has brought about the objective reconciliation and has provided humanity with the example of
reconciliation. Now that God has objectively liberated the oppressed from the finality of demonic clutches such as white
racism, oppressed humanity (African American people) must
assume its responsibility to fight consciously along with God
in Christ against injustice. Divine victory at Calvary and the

tomb objectively shattered the walls of hostility between white and black. Now the oppressed must act as if they are truly emancipated subjectively; that means fighting with total effort against white racism and for freedom. This is subjective reconciliation: that is to say, black folk organizing to overthrow the system of white supremacy and then to reconcile with white Americans. Therefore, Cone maintains the consistency of his liberation theme in both objective and subjective reconciliation.

For African Americans to bring about reconciliation, their task is fighting white oppression. For whites, reconciliation can only mean one thing — coming to God through black people, the place where Jesus is leading a movement for freedom.[17]

J. Deotis Roberts

Black Theology of Balance. Black power and the late 1960s freedom struggle by black America gave rise to Cone's theology. But J. Deotis Roberts (an ordained Baptist) started his intellectual ministry before this period. Roberts studied Christian Platonism during the 1950s at Edinburgh University in Scotland and Cambridge University in England. He became interested in European philosophy and faith, which he examined in his first two books (*Faith and Reason* [1962] and *From Puritanism to Platonism in Seventeenth Century England* [1968]).[18] Roberts's conversational partner was classical European-American philosophical theology. However, with urban rebellions flooding Dr. Martin Luther King's movement, Roberts began to respond theologically to the radical change in African American people's political scenery.

To understand Roberts's black theology, we have to see him as the product of two larger political developments — civil rights (from the mid-1950s to the mid-1960s) and black power (from the late 1960s to the mid-1970s). He and Dr. King finished their doctoral degrees around the same time in the 1950s. Both came out of a Southern Baptist environment which suggested that African Americans could improve their social status through hard work, impeccable educational credentials, and a reliance on Christian nonviolence. Eventually, a successful black achieved the reward of integration with white people. As a result, Roberts represents a particular black church tradition during the King and civil rights period. But while he was a professor at Howard University (Washington, D.C.), the political agitation and militancy of black power also directly affected him. In fact, he taught there while Stokely Carmichael was a student. Consequently, Roberts tried to combine the new ideas of the black power movement with the philosophy of King and the civil rights organizations.

Roberts, a member of the Society for the Study of Black Religion and distinguished professor of philosophical theology at the Eastern Baptist Theological Seminary (Wynnewood, Pennsylvania), set out to develop a black political theology. He was the third member of the black political theology group to publish a book (*Liberation and Reconciliation* [1971]).[19] Further situating himself with the political theologians, he explicitly named his second black theology book *A Black Political Theology* (1974).[20] But even in his controversial first work, we find his explanation of black political theology as a struggle between two *groups* of power systems:

> The reason why Black Theology is "political" is that the one-to-one approach is inadequate and unattractive to any black man who is aware of the serious and insidious character of racism.[21]

Within this theology, Roberts sets out a clear purpose which guides all of his theological writings. "What I am seeking," states Roberts, "is a Christian theological approach to race relations that will lead us beyond a hypocritical tokenism to liberation as a genuine reconciliation between equals."[22] He wants to combine liberation and reconciliation. Roberts feels that Cone has overemphasized liberation and has not taken seriously that reconciliation is what Jesus Christ calls for. So Roberts attempts to offer us a more realistic balance.

I describe Roberts's thinking as a black Christian theology of balance. He explains his *black* theology as "inner-city" theology reflecting upon black awareness and black power. It is *Christian* because he makes it equal with a "constructive restatement of the Christian faith" and sees the "raw material" for black theology as being in the African American church. Roberts describes his activity as *theology* because he emphasizes "reasoning about God." And he uses a theological methodology of *balance*. Referring to his theological outlook, Roberts summarizes:

> I tried to bridge the two generations of Dr. King and the one of the new black power and black consciousness movement.... My whole methodology and whole outlook would mean that I would almost have an equal balance. ... I'm on both sides of the fence.[23]

Roberts's writings have produced a controversy over whether or not he has handled correctly the Christian belief in liberation and reconciliation. Within the political trend of the first generation of black theologians, he states his fundamental belief here: "Thus I have spoken of ... liberation and reconciliation. A worthy Black Theology has to be balanced in this way."[24]

Liberation and Reconciliation. Within the black political theology trend, Cone will come to reconciliation after a redistribution of white political power. Roberts, in contrast, stands for black liberation against white racism and, simultaneously, for genuine reconciliation with white people. He targets liberation and reconciliation as the "twin goals" and "two main poles" of black theology.[25] Liberation calls for black people's freedom from the bondage of white racism. And reconciliation suggests that black freedom does not deny white humanity but meets whites on equal ground. Roberts seeks to develop both goals in a balanced way: that is, in terms of (1) always explaining one in relation to the other, and (2) using them as the core around which he weaves his systematic theology.

Christology. Roberts seeks to place Cone's christology in proper perspective. Cone believes Christ was never literally white and became black by his presence among the oppressed African American community. In *Liberation and Reconciliation,* Roberts states that he believes in a black Messiah, though not in a literal, historical sense. For him the black Messiah speaks to a psychocultural crisis. This crisis for African Americans comes about because white Christians have created a white Christ and say this god is the real and true picture of Jesus. African Americans suffer low self-esteem (e.g., psychological damage) when the God they worship is painted white and doesn't look like them. In addition, African Americans feel that their culture has no worth when they are on their knees looking up at a god which is only a portrait of a European male model. In Roberts's opinion, we must not limit Christianity to a white Christ. The black experience has to also be a major source for contemporary christology. A psychological need materializes to make Christ and the gospel address the black person directly. As a black image, Christ becomes one among African American people, and then the black person receives his or her own dignity and pride.

Furthermore, Roberts does not wish to demand that white Americans worship a black Christ. Thus Roberts does not call for a vengeful repentance from them for worshiping a white Christ. This type of "revenge" would dehumanize whites as they have done to African Americans. Besides, affirmation of a black Christ, for Roberts, includes room for a white Christ. But, applying his balanced methodology, if whites could overcome their superior-inferior state of mind and color consciousness and could worship a black Messiah, then reconciliation would be nearer.

Still, Roberts believes, real reconciliation through black and white equality would allow American blacks and whites to transcend the skin color of Christ and reach out to a "universal Christ" without color. At this point, Roberts answers the following questions: What is the relation between the black Messiah and the colorless Messiah? And what does this relationship have to do with liberation and reconciliation? The black Messiah is a symbol and a myth. In the African American experience, the black Messiah liberates blacks. At the same time, the universal Christ reconciles black and white Americans. Jesus Christ the liberator offers liberation from white oppression, provides forgiveness from sin, and delivers the African American community from exploitation. Jesus Christ the Reconciler brings black people together and black and white people together in "multiracial fellowship."

Roberts's *A Black Political Theology* book provides more information about his three dimensions of christology. (1) Christ operates both above human culture and in human culture while carrying out liberation for the whole person and speaking to the need for peoplehood. Christ is the focus of a theology of social change and political action. And Jesus is the liberator who goes wherever the oppressed are. (2) Along with "mainstream Protestantism," Roberts agrees that the *essence* or *substance* of christology lies in the universal Word — the lordship of Christ over each people. Black christology takes for granted this universal definition and puts it in the *form* of the African American experience. (3) Christ liberates us personally and from those things that confront our daily existence. And the universal Christ reconciles all Americans, black and white.[26]

Both James H. Cone and J. Deotis Roberts state that it is important to question the mainstream beliefs in theology. This type of theology, despite its claims, is not universal and does not reflect accurately the Bible and human social relations. In fact, white theology has found a home in institutions dominated by racism and white people's monopoly of power — that is, within the structures of higher education, the churches, and other institutions of the broader society. Both Cone and Roberts emphasize the relations between theology and power; that is to say, whites have monopolized power, and this monopolization is reflected in structures of white theology and in the marginalization of blacks. Yet the question remains: How does God affirm the beauty of blackness? This raises the issue of the role of culture in black theology.

Advocating a Faith Based in Black Culture

In the last half of this chapter we look at two representatives of the cultural theological trend of the first generation. Representatives of this group present a clear contrast to their political colleagues. From the perspective of the cultural trend, the black political theologians waste too much time and energy reacting to white racism while also accepting white definitions. In contrast, the cultural theologians distinguish themselves by condemning the white supremacist, cultural structure of religion and the discipline of white theology. They accuse the political theologians of waging an attack on European-American theology and religion while, at the same time, accepting a white intellectual framework.

In other words, the cultural teachers believe that African American Christians cannot get away from white supremacy if they continue to think like the Christian white supremacist. How can the black political theologian attack the racism in the discipline of theology while, at the same time, using the intellectual categories of white theology? We cannot defeat "the enemy" by thinking like "the enemy."

The cultural theologians call for a fundamental shift in the development of religion. To create or build this new religion, blacks need to also create or build new structures for this religion. In fact the cultural theologians do not want black Christians to spend a lot of time getting involved in the language "game" or structure of theology, because whites have created theology as an academic discipline for the benefit of white Christians. Consequently, African Americans need to move away from this "white" academic theology and focus on how they experience their own faith. To do this, black folk have to focus seriously on the African side of the African American reality. Using the categories of (1) black religious thought or language, (2) sources, (3) Africanisms, and (4) liberation, we look at the cultural theological perspectives of Gayraud S. Wilmore and Charles H. Long.

Gayraud S. Wilmore

Black Religious Thought. Gayraud S. Wilmore has had a major impact on contemporary black theology. Wilmore, an ordained Presbyterian, participated in the very early meetings of the ad hoc National Committee of Negro Churchmen (1966). He was one of the first to chair the committee's theological commission and shaped its pioneering black theological direction. Though trained in social ethics, Wilmore shifted emphasis to black history and black theology. His *Black Religion and Black Radicalism* (1972)[27] filled a major gap in the early black theological movement — the need for a fresh account of the many streams of resistance in African American religious history. The two volumes of *Black Theology: A Documentary History* (covering 1966–79 and 1980–92), which he co-edited with James Cone, are the classic textbooks on black theology.[28] Wilmore, a member of the Society for the Study of Black Religion, is retired from the Interdenominational Theological Center in Atlanta.

I refer to Wilmore's theology as black theology of religious thought. The phrase *religious thought* comes directly from his explanations of his writings. He wants to date any discussion of black theology long before the polemics against white theology of the 1960s. Furthermore, he evaluates theology within the general context of "black religious thought":

If we are going to talk about black theology, we really
need to go back to the beginning and not assume that
black theology began with the publication of Dr. Cone's
book in 1969. But when we do that, we have to agree
that we are not using theology in the strictly academic and
technical sense. What we really might use better is the term
... black religious thought.[29]

Wilmore argues for this description of black people's religious experience because he believes black *Christian* theology
grows out of black religious thought. He wants to dig deeper
because he discovers something broader beneath academic theology. Academic theology, in his opinion, mainly reflects the
confessions of the Christian church, the apostolic faith, the Old
and New Testaments, and church disciplines. Given the pri-
ority of black religious thought, how does Wilmore define
theology?

Black theology, Wilmore states, is not the mere opposite of
the dominant Christian theology, is not simply a black version
of white classical theology. On the contrary, black theology
becomes important when it uses specific black theological resources in order to bring about African American freedom.
Wilmore asks this question: In what ways do black Christian,
non-Christian, and *secular* groups comprehend, feel, and practice liberation as their final goal? Unpacking this final goal
is the theological work of black theology. When it does this,
continues Wilmore, black theology fulfills its proper task by
pointing the way toward the total black community's emancipation. Furthermore, the key to black theology is freedom for
African American people and, in that process, freedom for all
God's humanity.[30] Thus Wilmore works on a black theology
leaning more toward the liberation strands in non-Christian
black movements.

Even when we support the importance of black theology, we
still have to begin at the beginning, which is before the black

church. In that sense, Wilmore does not view theology as merely a church discipline. In his words:

> The seminal black theology of the African slaves on the plantations of the New World existed prior to the existence of the black church as such. Its first theologians were not theologically trained professors, but preacher-conjurers.[31]

Thus the roots of black theology not only go back to the historic African American church's resistance against slavery and racism but also extend to the attempts of all black secular and non-Christian groups to express the meaning and values of the black reality in the United States, Africa, and the Caribbean. Even today theology extends beyond the black church as a religious institution. It includes aspects of black life and culture, contends Wilmore, which white scholars would call secular, non-Christian, and sometimes anti-Christian.

Wilmore writes in order to create a new way of interpreting reality. He calls for a new pair of "eyes" for the African American community. How does the overall black community work toward its final goals and solutions in a situation of racist exploitation? For Wilmore, the key area is neither European-American theology nor simply black church documents. He searches the black oral tradition and literature, sifting through mythology, ethical norms, and folklore. There he discovers black religious thought.[32]

Sources. Black religious thought becomes the umbrella and backdrop for a black theology. Black theology is only one part of this larger religious experience of the African American community. Offering a much broader perspective, Wilmore moves black religious thought from the narrow issues found in a systematic church theology to the many and varied religious experiences of the masses of African American people. For the entire community, black religious thought is held together by a basic reality: an indestructible belief in freedom, a freedom born in the African environment. This informal religious thought of black folk, therefore, opens up a whole new world of sources with which to sharpen a new black interpretation for liberation. As long as belief in freedom is at the center of all black sources, following Wilmore's line of reasoning, we can use any part of African American culture to develop our theology, as long as God's spirit of liberation is part of the culture. The possibilities of black cultural, theological creativity seem endless.

In *Black Religion and Black Radicalism,* Wilmore uncovers three locations for theological sources.[33] He does not directly include scripture and early church tradition in his three sources. He assumes that the Bible and church tradition are obvious sources, and he thus deemphasizes them in the development of his black religious thought. Wilmore appears to promote non-Christian resources.

The first source he highlights is the lower-class black community's folk religion. In his judgment, black faith as folk religion has been the motor for all major revolutionary and nationalist mass-based movements of blacks. And it has also kept alive some parts of Africa's cultural importance for black America. Sometimes folk religion overlaps the black Christian church. Other times it unfolds in movements like the Nation of Islam, Marcus Garvey's efforts, black Islam, black Judaism, the Azusa Street Revival, and Daddy Grace.

The second source is the "writings, sermons, and addresses of the black preachers and public men and women of the past." Wilmore agrees that not all historical black heroines and heroes were members of the clergy. But he claims that almost all these heroines and heroes experienced religious conditioning from the black community. They reflected the unique spirituality of African American life and culture. Both the black clergy and the black cultural artists have drawn on the religious and theological themes of suffering, struggle, hope, justice, faith, survival, and liberation of black people. Therefore, we must also look for theological implications in the essays of Alice Walker, the poetry of Countee Cullen, the novels of Richard Wright, and the tales of Langston Hughes. For Wilmore, we do not develop black theology primarily in white seminaries. Black theology is found "in the streets, in taverns and pool halls, as well as in churches."

Traditional religions of Africa make up the third source of black theology. Wilmore instructs us to remember the long history of African Americans; black people are an *African* people. Consequently, the religious and theological connections to ancient and modern Africa have a big impact on contemporary black knowledge of God. The particular way God revealed God's self in precolonial Africa contributes to the survival and liberation of black people on both sides of the Atlantic. A modification of African traditional religious beliefs, values, and practices could very well bring about a rebirth of African American religion in North America. Here Wilmore also calls for a cooperative venture between black Americans and Africans to rediscover and uncover common "belief structures and worship practices" in black religious norms and traditions.

Wilmore believes that any future work on black theology has to go back to the period of African American life in slavery. I include this as his fourth and final source. During slavery, various theological and religious themes came together to make up the basis of black religious thought. The following shows Wilmore's position on the black cultural elements in slavery-based black religion:

> In the formation of a new common language, in the telling of animal tales and proverbs, in the leisure time practice of remembered handicrafts, in the preparation of foods, homemade medicines, and magical potions and charms, in the standardization of rituals of birth, marriage, and death, in the creation of modes of play and parody, in the expression of favorite styles of singing, instrumental music, and the dance,...the slaves wove for themselves the tapestry of a new African-American culture.[34]

These unified cultural aspects were integrated into a basic religious conception of life and reality. To find out why and how black Christians and the entire black community look at the world in a religious way, we have to go back to the cultural elements just mentioned. In the unique ways in which African American culture formed itself, we discover the plain theology of black religious thought. Africanisms were key elements in that culture, elements we thus need to examine.

Africanisms. Theologians who emphasize black cultural trends unanimously agree that Africanisms (i.e., conscious and unconscious memories of Africa) occupy a prominent role in black religion and, therefore, in the construction of an authentic black theology of liberation. They advocate giving more attention to the religious implications of the (conscious or unconscious) memory of African values and worldviews. Wilmore points to several religious themes that he believes survive from Africa in today's black community: (1) No sharp separation exists between the secular and the sacred, religion and life. (2) Religion is practical. It relates directly to food, shelter, economic life, child rearing, and recreation. Religion must work in everyday life. (3) As in Africa, the overall black community places a premium on family, solidarity, and communalism as opposed to excessive individualism. (4) Black folk worship God with the fullness of their bodies, minds, and spirits. This links to liberation because the Spirit descends and liberates both the soul and the body. "The same Spirit which calls us out of the rigidity of our psychosomatic entity, calls us out of the tyranny of our political bondage." For Wilmore, the doctrine of the Spirit includes the freeing of the body and the soul. (5) When the black community speaks of the presence of God and the Spirit in its midst, this indicates the spirit of black ancestors' lives.[35]

With these religious Africanisms, Wilmore wishes to carry out a correction of the "whitenization of black religion." Africanisms point to the fact that God, the Lord of all people and cultures, created Africanness in "black Americans." As God-created, Africanisms inherently contain creative, positive theological value for black people and all humanity. In brief, they contain possibilities for liberation.

Liberation. To understand Wilmore's theological conception of liberation or freedom, we have to keep in mind his attraction to African culture. Wilmore describes how the move toward religious freedom on the part of the black masses actually grew out of their past African environment. In this earlier African situation, freedom pointed to real deliverance on earth, liberation from all powers that blocked the holistic freedom of mind, body, and spirit. Any power that tried to stop the full advancement of the individual in community would be defeated. At this point, Wilmore emphasizes that liberation stands for more than politics and economics. It means

> freedom of the person as a child of God, the freedom to
> be himself and herself most fully, to realize the most cre-
> ative potential of his or her psychophysical nature.... The
> freedom that black religion celebrates and black theology
> seeks to explicate is simply the freedom to be a child of
> God.[36]

For Wilmore, freedom in the theological sense is each individual of the community reaching the height of his or her God-given possibilities. We achieve divinely initiated liberation once we reach the fullest potential of our mind and body. Divine freedom produces full human creativity; therefore, blocking human wholeness attacks divine purpose.

Wilmore sees a necessity to talk in theological language about black people's final goal of liberation because of the origin of black folk's yearning for liberation. Liberation comes from African Americans' natural consciousness of a transcendent reality. In that reality freedom combined with the essence of the definition of humanity, a humanity that is created in *the image of God.*[37] Thus in addition to being a *child* of God and reaching full *wholeness,* an African American person undergoes a liberated experience with the complete realization of God's *image* in her or him. In fact, attaining maximum human potential mirrors the divine image. God created humanity to be human in the fullest sense of the word. To be human is to succeed in all that is humanly possible. For black Americans, then, there is an African religious and cultural sense that human creativity contains God's image.

Furthermore, liberation shows us God's command, a mandated theological ethic, to practice right choices. The black Christian community, Wilmore writes, needs to regain "a sense of cultural vocation that relates to their experience of struggle in terms of both spiritual formation and social transformation."[38] Wilmore's use of the phrase "cultural vocation" pinpoints at least two things. First, liberation does not come from a whimsical human decision about what to do in life. On the contrary, the divine calls and puts before humanity the vocation — a lifelong pursuit in response to God's word — to be free.

Second, spiritual formation and social change come together in a vocation of culture. Culture acts as the umbrella for the holistic liberation of the spirit and body. Wilmore's preference for culture as the context for politics becomes clear in this instance. For him, to see liberation primarily in political terms would narrow black people's religious way of life to a political liberation in reaction to whites, whereas culture, as he uses it, expresses a total mind-body-spirit religious way of believing and doing. A cultural perspective seems to imply a proactive black religious style of being.

Though he gives preference to culture, Wilmore does indeed recognize the connection between political and cultural liberation. Yet he avoids a one-sided goal of only political liberation because he believes that it yields an incomplete and deformed result. In Wilmore's view, we cannot reach the fullest measure of human liberation while remaining captive to the oppressor's culture. People have "to appreciate and value their own traditions in art and music and literature and family life and childrearing habits and recreation and all the multiplex aspects of human life."[39] The African American community does not engage in these cultural activities as an idle pastime.

Again, for Wilmore, in these very activities, that is, in culture, one identifies sources of religious and theological values held over from Africa. Until black folks appreciate the cultural way, and thus the religious way, political liberation is only half a victory: African American people would win the political battle but lose the overall cultural (religious and theological) war to their white oppressors. Thus only with success in the cultural sphere will black liberation give us a thoroughgoing victory over demonic principalities and powers on earth.

Charles H. Long

Black Religious Language. Throughout the 1970s, Charles H. Long waged an outspoken struggle against attempts at creating a black theology and neglecting the primacy of culture in African American life and religion. Past president of the American Academy of Religion and member of the Society for the Study of Black Religion, Long does not usually call himself a black theologian. On the contrary, he did his formal studies in the history of religions. Indeed, his discipline affects directly his interpretation of black theology. Therefore a look at his definition of history and religion will aid in understanding his position:

> By "history" I mean the particular temporal-spatial cultural situation in which man responds to that which is sacred and by "religion" I mean the structure of the myth, symbol, or religious response through which man apprehends the sacred. The historian of religion is interested in understanding the enduring structure of these responses.[40]

History is human culture, and human culture is the place for humanity's response to the sacred. Put differently, the place of human activity and connection with the holy is culture. Culture gives birth to religion. And religion gives us structures so that we can understand the presence of the holy. Here Long hopes to avoid the error of simply adopting white people's religious structures — a mistake African Americans have often made. Rather, he targets the very (white) religious structure itself. He wants to remove this European way of thinking (i.e., white structures) and build new black ways of thinking (i.e., black structures) from something religiously new.

Long agrees with Wilmore's emphasis on the need to broaden black religious thought to include non-Christian and secular experiences. Long complements Wilmore's work by using a unique definition of religious language. In fact, I call Long's perspective a black religious language.

First, he defines religion as the fountainhead out of which all other important realities, including theology, emerge. "For my purposes," he writes, "religion will mean orientation — orientation in the ultimate sense, that is, how one comes to terms with the ultimate significance of one's place in the world."[41] Religion, then, deals with how a group decides on its final goals in a cultural time and space. Thus the *entire* African American community is religious because it confronts the question of ultimate significance or the final goal. As a result, all languages come out of religion — language about God, salvation, and creation.

Next, language has a specific meaning for Long. In a certain sense language does not mirror reality; language is all of reality. "All you have is language," comments Long. He continues:

> There is nothing behind, before, underneath, overarching or whatever. So whatever reality you want to talk about is in the language.... So that language has its own materiality. It is not so much that there is a reality there and I'm using these words just to say what I want to say about it. I am saying that in language is the reality that I am

expressing....I do not think language is just something
that represents something else.[42]

Here one can better grasp the fundamental problem Long
has with the meaning and origin of language. He does not see
religious language as a flimsy shadow of some other real religious substance. Language is not like a mirror which only
reflects back a picture of something else which is real. Religious
language *is* religious substance. In his perspective, languages express power when they support the way of life and structures of
the people who speak the language.

Therefore, genuine black religious language is the actual and
concrete expression of what takes place within African American culture and life. Black language is the real black life, not
a reflection. Either black folk develop their own language and
structures for this new language, or African Americans will have
to accept the language of white Christians. If they imitate white
language, African Americans will be agreeing to be controlled
by whites.

With his definition of religion and language, Long is against
black theology because he believes theology started and pres-
ently acts as a "power discourse" used by the white oppressor
in that oppressor's interests. Long attacks the very structure
(as opposed to reinterpreting theological categories) of theology because theology represents a language of those (white)
people who have the power to define cultural categories. African American people and poor people, argues Long, have not
had the privilege of establishing cultural categories. Thus why
should black people enter the "imitative game" of saying they
will attain their liberation by talking and acting like those who
have oppressed them? Again, theology is white people's power
language.

Relatedly, and similar to Wilmore, Long has a major problem with black theology because, in his words, "it is church
theology." Yet in Long's opinion, churches only include that

segment of black religion and culture that calls itself Christian. In fact, the African American community also includes a great deal of other religious elements that have final goals or ultimate concerns. By naming themselves advocates of black theology, African American religious intellectuals and clergy miss the non-Christian types of religion in black culture. As a result, theology and black theology, in particular, narrow the categories of religious language in the African American community.[43]

Using the same reasoning, Long cautions against accepting Christianity as an authentic religion for the liberation of black religious language. He states that Christianity is probably the only religion that has a theology. Why? Because "Christianity is not a grassroots religion... that grows up out of the ground of the people."[44] Even when Christianity spread across Europe, some other type of religious language was already present. Long points out that wherever Christianity arrived throughout the world, the people were already practicing a different and vibrant cultural and religious life. In short, both theology and Christianity operate as dominating power languages. And so we need other sources for black religious language.

Sources. Long approaches sources in order to answer this question: What are the religious elements in the cultural experience of black folk? He contrasts his approach to the major representative of the black theological political trend, James H. Cone. Cone, for Long, functions essentially as an "apologetic [theologian] working implicitly and explicitly from the Christian theological tradition." Cone has accepted the theological structure of the Christian religious language. Long then raises the shortcomings of the methodology of apologetic theology. "This limitation of methodological perspectives" on the part of Cone, Long states, has resulted in a narrow understanding and the exclusion of certain creative possibilities among African American people.[45]

Long turns his eye toward the more vitally important expressions forthcoming from the black community itself. There we begin with the raw data of black religious language, which include Christians and non-Christians. For example, Long "would spend as much time with Count Basie, Jimmy Lungford, and Cab Calloway, and black poets, and all these kind of folks as I would with ministers." He includes other such notables as Carter G. Woodson, W. E. B. Du Bois, George Washington Carver, and Jelly Roll Morton.[46] Both ministers and nonministers struggle to give religious meaning to black life and experience. The nonministers occupy a position in black religious language just as creative and just as powerful as that of the ministers.

Long's religious and theological sources fall into four groups.[47] Agreeing with Wilmore, he first points out the involuntary presence of black people, who are Africa's descendants in America. When the first Africans arrived in the New World, the process of creating black Americans began. Involuntary presence proved and continues to prove key to that creation. Slavery had to have affected in a unique way how enslaved Africans (and today's black community) viewed their final goals (i.e., that which was holy for them). Therefore involuntary presence and orientation communicate deep-seated religious meaning. Slaves experienced negativity in bondage and, at the same time, created a different reality from a unique perception of their final goals. During slavery, the enslaved African and African American changed and created their experience of God or the holy by using their own religious consciousness.

Like Wilmore, Long also looks for the African American community's experience with the holy in tradition, a second source. The oral tradition of black folklore offers a gold mine of creative religious possibilities. What does a combing of slave narratives, black sermons, the words and music of the spirituals and the blues, and the cycle of Br'er Rabbit and High John the Conqueror stories tell us about religious consciousness? "These materials reveal," Long writes, "a range of religious meanings extending from trickster-transformer hero to High Gods."

In addition, slaves adopted and put new meaning into the biblical imagery of the Bible, a third source. They interpreted God's deliverance of Israel from Egyptian bondage, Long states, as a sign of hope. Furthermore, the slaves saw God as the omnipotent, moral deity who held power to set things right. And the slaves never or hardly ever accused God in situations of suffering. For example, in order to maintain their humanity and dignity when confronted with the majority population's acts of white supremacy, slaves experienced the biblical God as a "transformer of their consciousness."

In particular, Long examines the slaves' stories about their conversion events and discovers a combination of a practical "God acting in history" and a concern for "mystification of consciousness." In these conversion stories, the appearance of God overwhelms the slaves within the reality of the black religious experience, not in terms of the trinitarian dogma of Father–Son–Holy Ghost. Accordingly, these theological structures (of how God acts in ordinary events and transforms religious consciousness) can give us clues about black religious consciousness for the entire African American community. In other words, the slaves' sense of the God who acts and transforms in the Christian conversion experience is also found in the religious consciousness of non-Christian movements like "the Black Muslims and the Black Jews."

Enslaved black folk also saw some difference between God and Jesus Christ. Consequently, Long admits that to the extent blacks have believed in Christianity, language about the Trinity has appeared. However, for African Americans, the Trinity became real in their practice of religion on a daily basis and not in dogma and doctrine. The slaves simply experienced Jesus as another form of God, not as the abstract second person of the Trinity. Particularly in biblical stories, Christ acted in various ways which helped the slaves to survive. For them, the Christ of the Bible became a fellow sufferer, a little child, a companion and person who understands. Long sees the essence of Jesus' religious identity in Jesus' role of companion and creator, "a deity related more to the human condition than deities of the sky and the subjection of this deity to death at the hands of men."

Also reflecting Wilmore's concern, the image and historical reality of Africa make up Long's final source. Admittedly, the system of white supremacy caused brutal actions during slavery which did splinter and thus affect adversely whatever cultural forms Africans brought with them from their home continent. Yet, Long states, one cannot overlook the ebbing and flowing of the image and historical reality of Africa within the religious consciousness of black Americans since they were brought to the "New World" in 1619. More specifically, the image and the reality have shown themselves in African American dance, music, and political theory. Thus, part of black folk's Ultimate Concern is the feeling of not having a real home. On the one hand, black existence is an American existence, suggests Long. On the other hand, being black in America means being forced from one's original home in Africa and then trying to set up a new home in the U.S. This produces an instinctive yearning for a connectedness to the Continent, a desire to relate to Africa.

Africanisms. Long defines an Africanism as a kind of orientation toward and way of looking at reality. He claims this method of grasping and looking at reality has probably carried over from Africa to black America. Africans came to the New World shores with their own religious beliefs and rituals. They were not empty heads and without imagination. Despite white acts of cruelty in breaking up families and forbidding the speaking of African languages — all aimed at cultural domination — the African worldview, and thus the perspective of African languages, continued to exist. Since Long describes religion as orientation toward one's Ultimate Concern or final goal in life (i.e., the holy), he sees black people's African understanding of the world as having religious importance.

For example, though West Africa includes different peoples and languages, underneath this difference lies a structural unity found in religious and linguistic forms. A great majority of American slaves originated in West Africa, and this meant that a vast majority of the slaves shared a sense of these common forms. When European and white American slavers attempted to stop Africans from speaking in their own African languages and cultural styles, this commonality persisted, as did the religious structures and patterns the slaves brought with them from Africa. Long mentions the example of shout songs on the part of slaves, their secret meetings for "conjuring," and the continued presence of African rhythm and dance in American culture.

However, Long's major focus for his study of Africanisms appears to be the religious implications of the image of Africa in the minds of slaves. Even if the slave could not directly remember Africa, the imprint of Africa's image stuck as a place of historical origin. Brutally removed from their homeland, Africans still maintained an unconscious or conscious memory of Africa which stood for their beginning, like a form of creation. Theologically, the image of Africa presents these questions for Long: Does the forced removal of black folk from their homeland indicate a specific divine purpose with strategic implications? (This question calls up parallels to the Hebrew people's traveling in the wilderness on the way to Canaan.) Are African Americans on the way to a land of milk and honey? Are they to reconnect to their sisters and brothers on the Continent to help in their God-ordained freedom?

Or perhaps, as a remnant of God's purpose on earth, black Americans must bear the burden of taking the lead and changing America into what God has created all humankind to become. Is the purpose of African Americans to help overcome the tower of Babel cultural wars in the United States and establish the harmonious unity of diverse American cultures "speaking in tongues" about the same God? Long's exploration of the image and history of Africa opens up further religious avenues filled with theological possibilities.

Long's religious and historical image-structure of Africa in black religious consciousness also touches on eschatological hope (i.e., the future and long-term hope) for black Americans. The religious and symbolic value of land (Africa) — a value that can be carried in the spirit and mind — implies that it is unnecessary to actually return to the African continent, in the sense of massive Pan-African migration. Yet a clear imprint of Africa in the religious consciousness could provide a foundation for the future potential of African American freedom. The knowledge that God created a black lineage from a definite land could imply that the movement toward independence and wholeness in Africa has a direct link to black America. Since God moves in mysterious ways in African liberation, cannot and will not God move in a similar manner by giving freedom to the same blood and flesh of Africans in America? Africa might be the model for African American liberation.[48]

Liberation. Understanding what Long sees as the target of liberation helps us appreciate his understanding of liberation. Long charges European-Americans with carrying out a second creation in the case of black communities in America: "The oppressed must deal with...the fictive truth of their status as expressed by the oppressors, that is, their second creation."[49] The West created black America out of the West's own history and language. Africa's descendants would not be in the United States, asserts Long, if Europeans had not brought them here. Since Africans' arrival, whites have continued to define what it means to be black in white America. The dominant America, then, used its cultural language, its way of looking at reality, and its practice of religion to make blacks invisible. Referring to the European conquest of African slaves (and Native Americans), Long asserts: "The economic and military conquest was accomplished, but another conquest more subtle and with even longer-lasting effects had taken place. This was the linguistic conquest."[50]

Within the conquest of language, theology is an oppressive system that prevents African Americans from having their own black cultural meaning. Usually, theology functions like an imperialistic language system. Along with Christianity, it superimposes itself upon preexisting religious structures. When it arrives in a country or community for the first time, it smothers and covers up other religions that were already in existence before the arrival of Christianity.

The artificial, second creation by European cultural practices comes after the first creation, the work of God. Thus African American people's struggle for liberation has been to reaffirm their truth and autonomy given in the first creation. In a sense, black liberation resides in black people renaming themselves in accord with the first creation. Admittedly, they cannot actually return to the beginnings. Therefore, liberation, in the long term, should bring about a third creation, God's new creation of a new humanity.[51]

Liberation will come with a new language, Long reasons, not just in regard to its content and semantics, but in the essence of its structure, rhythm, and texture. A liberative language helps humanity to become human in the world. For instance, because of the physical restrictions of slavery, Africans could not physically carry out actions of change. They had to imagine those actions, and thus the locus of change became the religious consciousness. Thus new and liberative language must be situated in the religious consciousness, which is the orientation toward ultimate concern (i.e., the holy).

In addition to liberation in new language and the religious consciousness, African Americans' fight for their God-created humanity takes the form of validating cultural identity. Long asserts: "A great deal of the fight for human rights [by African Americans] is not only economic but a fight for the legitimation of Black cultural forms — those that have survived from Africa and those created in America."[52]

Part of African Americans' struggle for their humanity is believing that God has created black culture, and that belief necessitates a return to the African American past. It necessitates an intellectual and cultural investigation. Long calls for a project to clarify the meanings of "those strange, profound, comical and sober deposits of [black folk's] past." This effort has major implications. If we fail to interpret those parts of black history, then it means perpetual slavery. Therefore, those deposits "must be vindicated or we shall never be free."[53]

Pursuing liberation in cultural identity, Long has proposed a study to look at the connections between different religious traditions in the United States. In the dialogue, each tradition would hold equal status with no one assuming "the normative structure of discourse." Culture would be the focus of the investigation, and the participants would use a "hermeneutic of deciphering." Such an equal give-and-take might reveal a new, genuine structure of religious meaning for America.[54]

Remembering Long's description of language possessing its own substance and reality, we can see how an important conversation created from equality and liberation could bring about a new religious relation among America's cultural groups. Because language is real, different people sharing their languages equally means we are moving closer to equal social relations among all peoples.

Conclusion

The cultural theologians examined above insisted on redefining theology, an insistence that has greatly helped the movement for black freedom. Seeking a more inclusive theology than that of the political trend's church theology, the cultural group includes religious examples from the entire black community. If any black person hopes and fights for freedom, then the forms that hope and struggle take are elements of black theology of liberation. The cultural theologians review black history and correctly perceive diverse radical strands, both church and nonchurch.

In addition, the cultural trend advises the African American community to rely on black cultural foundations. These theologians believe correctly that a liberating black theology has to stay close to the God-given resources in the African American community. The question becomes: How is a liberating black faith shown in black culture, history, and a total black way of life? We have to agree with the cultural theologians: God has revealed God's self in sources unique to black Americans.

God also is present in black reality by not allowing a complete break in African lineage. African American people have a rich heritage in the African side of their black American existence. The cultural trend links insightfully and persuasively the 1960s black theology movement to Africa's religious concepts. These theologians know very well that today's black faith blossoms from an African root. Thus a person reaches self-awareness through remembering his or her historical and foundational experiences.

God likewise has provided a different black religious and cultural structure for dealing with life and black folk's divine interaction with God. Cultural theologians explore the rhythm and texture of black faith's language structure. They raise important issues: What impact does black religious language have on black life? Does the syntax and cadence of black talk about God affect black folk's faith perception of God in their daily activities? Is singing an important part of black liberation theology?

On the other hand, the political theological group's strength is its clear recognition of the decisive role and impact of the black church, historically and today, in the survival and liberation of African American spiritual and material humanity. Therefore, the political group is correct in stressing the importance of reflecting systematically and critically on the nature of the vocation to which the African American church is called to preach and witness. It was the enslaved black people's church (i.e., the secret Invisible Institution) which laid the foundation for the language, religious, cultural, spiritual, and psychological beliefs and practices of most of black America.

Even today, the African American church offers the best opportunity to mobilize and organize huge sections of the black community for the struggle for its full spiritual and material humanity, a state ordained by God but blocked by visible and invisible structures of evil. Moreover, we could argue that even African American nonchurchgoers are impacted by the faith, tradition, and leadership of the black church. Even if the impact is negative, it testifies to the necessity and centrality of black church presence in the heart of the geographic black community and in the symbolic heart of African American people.

Because of the black church's tradition and potentiality, the political theologians are correct in using the discipline of systematic theology to critically question the church and to remind it of its prophetic calling for the full spiritual and material liberation of the poor.

The cultural and political trends contrast and complement each other. They both begin with God's involvement in black liberation and black freedom from white oppression and white theology. From these issues of black and divine freedom, political theologians move to confront harmful white power-relations in systems. From the same issues, their cultural colleagues move toward a focus on blackness. Both trends include politics and culture. The political theme unites with the cultural but asks how a singular emphasis on culture assists God's movement against white power-structures. The cultural thrust, in turn, agrees with political struggle but questions how this aids God's movement in and validation of blackness. Each fills in what the other lacks.

Chapter 3

The Second Generation

As noted earlier, two developments — the 1966 statement in the *New York Times* by the National Committee of Negro Churchmen and the publication of James H. Cone's *Black Theology and Black Power* in the spring of 1969 — symbolized a radical shift in theological studies and started the first generation of black theologians in the contemporary period of African American religious scholarship.[1]

The seeds of these two events have produced the fruit of a second generation of black theologians. The rise of this second group was marked by the appearance of two 1979 articles by younger writers. The first, "Black Theology and Black Women," was by Jacquelyn Grant (a systematic theologian), and the second, "Black Theology and Marxist Thought," was by Cornel West (a twenty-six-year-old philosopher of religion).[2] Both scholars affirmed the groundbreaking role, vital necessity, and theological creativity of the first generation. But, at the same time, Grant and West raised strong criticisms and challenges.

For instance, Grant accused black theology of maintaining the invisibility of African American women. How could black theology raise the banner of liberation when black women suffered from pains of gender discrimination? Black theology was really African American men talking about themselves because God's relation to black women was not present in black men's writings. Likewise, but from Marxist philosophical criticism, West implied the irrelevance of black theology if poor and working-class people and democratic socialism were not taken seriously. If black poor people and their lack of ownership of the wealth of America were not at the center of the discussion in black theology, then black theology was not for God and liberation. On the contrary, it was in favor of capitalism, which is nothing but exploitation. Clearly, new voices were posing strong questions about the health of the entire black theological process.

Following on the 1979 articles by Grant and West, in the 1980s and 1990s a group of young African American scholars branched out into a variety of black theological concerns. On the one hand, they have sought to pursue the first generation's pioneering agenda. On the other hand, they also have claimed their own distinct approaches. In a word, the second generation are both heirs to the black theological founders and groundbreakers in their own right.

Womanist Theology

Before moving on to the intellectual developments of the second generation as a whole, it is important here to briefly point to the distinct and creative work of womanists (i.e., black female religious scholars and clergy women). In line with Jacquelyn Grant's 1979 critique, the womanists have asserted boldly their presence and their right to think theologically from the particular perspectives and unique activities of African American women. Using various disciplines, some representative works are Katie G. Cannon's *Black Womanist Ethics* (1988), Renita J. Weems's *Just a Sister Away: A Womanist Vision of Women's Relationships in the Bible* (1988), and Grant's *White Women's Christ and Black Women's Jesus* (1989).[3] In contrast to the first- and second-generation (male) writers, womanists have held together consistently issues of gender, race, class, sexual orientation, and, to a certain degree, ecology. Differing from both white feminists and black male theologians, womanists' primary theological norm is how the spirit of liberation shows itself in all the parts of black women's and the entire African American community's experience.

Even more, they are less tied down by the constraints of "orthodox" (read: European-American and male) doctrines. Indeed, because of their listening to whatever black women say and do in their religious experiences, black female scholars have created a newness in their talk about God. For instance, Delores S. Williams has looked into literary fiction (in her "Black Women's Literature and the Task of Feminist Theology") and named "a language of the spirit" (in her "Womanist Theology: Black Women's Voices").[4] And it is this spirit talking that has taken the women beyond boundaries, out to the margins, back into the mainstream, and wherever they want to go in the church, society, the Bible, and educational institutions for discovering their own voice.

Moreover, Williams's *Sisters in the Wilderness: The Challenge of Womanist God-Talk* uses the biblical figure of Hagar, an African woman, to explore the unity and difference between womanist theology and white feminist theology, as well as to raise questions about the harmful nature of mainstream theological ideas concerning suffering as these ideas apply to African American women. In this same book, she raises the question of whether a belief in survival and quality of life should be more central to black theology than the belief in liberation.[5]

The unity of black women scholars and clergy women, however, has not led womanists to a false, peaceful coexistence. On the contrary, just as they apply a rigorous criticism to black men, so too do they engage in creative and sharp differences among themselves. Some of their unities and distinctions over what constitutes "womanist" can be found in "Roundtable Discussion: Christian Ethics and Theology in Womanist Perspectives."[6] Thus African American women religious leaders seem to hope for a womanist theology which (1) includes all pains, (2) is scholarly yet accessible to the broader society,

(3) is collegial, but not uncritical toward black men, and (4) is grounded on the black tradition, while continually renewing itself. Because of the significance of womanist theology, I give a more comprehensive analysis in the following chapter.

Intellectual Developments

The concerns of second-generation black male theologians and religious scholars can be classified into several broad categories: popular culture, the black poor folk, Afrocentricity, remaking traditional disciplines from a black perspective, global connections, questioning black theology's claims of liberation, and interdisciplinary approaches to black theology.

Popular Culture

The term "popular culture" here refers to a particular way of life of African American people or significant sectors of that population. It includes works of artists and intellectuals which are accepted widely by black folk or large parts of that group. It is a way of life: of talking, walking, singing, dancing, thinking, seeing, and acting out the black reality in America. Moreover, though this type of way of life and these artistic and intellectual expressions might be mass-produced and commercialized, they come mostly from nonelite culture and from culture which is seen as ignorant, animalistic, or simple-minded by the dominant U.S. population. Thus black popular culture encompasses, among other factors, a unique African American art form, a style of current events, reenacted folk wisdom, an intentional ebony self-identity, a black ebonics language, and the ritual practices emerging from below, from the folk at the bottom, from black daily life. It is the popularized words and practices of African Americans today.[7]

Drawing on popular culture, a group of black theologians

has created a new discipline called "theomusicology." Their journal, *Black Sacred Music: A Journal of Theomusicology,* published by Duke University Press, is devoted to scholarly writings in the areas of black sacred and secular music from a theological perspective. The journal's editor, Jon Michael Spencer, defines theomusicology as

> a theologically informed discipline,...a musicological method for theologizing about the sacred (the religious/ churched), the secular (the theistic unreligious/unchurched), and the profane (the atheistic/irreligious) — including sacred and nonsacred music functioning as theomusico-therapy in church and community — principally incorporating methods borrowed from anthropology, sociology, psychology, and philosophy.[8]

Using some traditional African theologies, theomusicology sees the presence of the divine in all parts of life without a false separation between sacred and secular. Similarly, it is multidisciplinary in approach, with music serving a healing role for oppressed people. Indeed, the fall 1989 edition of *Black Sacred Music* includes, among others, black theomusicological views on the blues, jazz (Thelonius Monk), the music of black power (James Brown), African American God-talk and "sexual healing" (Marvin Gaye), black musical eroticism (Prince), and "a postmodern Afro-American secular spirituality" (Michael Jackson). Basically, the theomusicological emphasis combines black theology, cultural criticism, the social sciences and philosophy, and a radical journey into mass popular culture. Spencer's *Protest and Praise: Sacred Music of Black Religion* was the first book using the theomusicological tool.[9]

Another instance of popular culture, this time centering on liberation ethics, is Garth Baker-Fletcher's *Xodus: An African American Male Journey,*[10] which seeks to make black churches and black Christians take seriously the crisis of opportunity and self-image faced by black males. Drawing on lessons from Martin Luther King Jr., Malcolm X, Howard Thurman, womanist theologians, the "new male" movement of white males, black male myths, commonsense folk wisdom, popular writings about diverse classes in the black community, and, perhaps most important, rap activists or "raptivists," Baker-Fletcher maps the black male's journey into new and healthy male space, particularly psychospiritual liberation. Such an event of the mind and the spirit involves a movement from Euro-American desires to African-focused ways of life, beliefs, and rituals. Baker-Fletcher summarizes his project in this way:

> This new thing [i.e., the mind-set of today's black American] is a resurrection of African-centered consciousness — Afrocentricity. It has not been fashioned, systematized, and intellectualized by academics but is arising creatively out of the twisted remains of urban uprisings, the shattered bodies of drive-by shooting victims, and the angry voices shouting "No Justice, No Peace!" A kind of revolution is happening, described by rappers with a back-burner beat of hip-hop rhythm, moving the minds, bodies, and feet of the masses away from the control of the system toward a new place.[11]

A theological ethic (e.g., characterized by liberation, inclusiveness, and solidarity) appropriate for our times, argues Baker-Fletcher, will help in the creation of the new Xodus male self who performs self-empowerment, joins with black women, and loves the children and the folk. *Xodus* expresses the urgency of contemporary black rap activists regarding the crisis and opportunities for all African American males, but especially black youth as an endangered species "in the streets."

Black Poor Folk

After popular culture, the next development in the second generation is relying on the religious experiences of black poor folk.

If black theology is to remain a liberation conversation and practice, then it must be based in and driven by the poor sectors of the African American community, both men and women. What do these people say about theology and ethics and their construction? Does God speak through and work with them?

To begin to answer such questions, Riggins R. Earl Jr. has written *Dark Symbols, Obscure Signs: God, Self, and Community in the Slave Mind*. It is about a way of relying on the poor for a proactive black theology of liberation.[12] Earl draws on ex-slave interviews, folk culture, and the spirituals to assess how illiterate poor African Americans have built the founding structures for a contemporary black theology and ethics. These foremothers and forefathers of today's black theology created four types of narratives to develop a healthy black self: soul narrative, the rational narrative, the playful narrative, and the dialogical narrative. And all four alternatives worked together to serve black people's unique experience of God, self, and community.

This approach toward poor folk also appears in the book *Cut Loose Your Stammering Tongue: Black Theology in the Slave Narratives,* edited by George C. L. Cummings and myself.[13] The contributors to the book draw on some of the forty-one volumes of interviews with ex-slaves and one hundred slave autobiographies which remain barely touched by African American theologians. *Cut Loose* brings together male and female scholars who engage slave narratives from the perspectives of theological doctrine, biblical studies, hermeneutics, phenomenology, and ethics. As the introduction to this volume states, the collaborators hope to develop further "a method of African American theology and black religion where the *main* resource for black action and talk about God arises out of the lives and words of *poor* black people's faith."

My book *Shoes That Fit Our Feet: Sources for a Constructive Black Theology* continues the call for engagement with the faith and life of poor, illiterate blacks.[14] This work discusses a black theological exploration of slave religion, poor black women's faith found in Toni Morrison's fiction, the unorthodox theology of African American folk culture, the political and religious beliefs of W. E. B. Du Bois, and the faith-based concerns in Martin Luther King's and Malcolm X's radical social analyses and transformative visions. The book calls for baptizing a black theology of liberation in the environment of those who not only lack a voice but, in certain instances, cannot read or write. Furthermore, the final chapter offers a schematic outline for a constructive black theology of liberation. Specifically, it presents three guidelines, four relationships, and four types of disciplines out of which a contemporary black theology can be developed.[15]

Finally, Joseph A. Brown, in his *To Stand on the Rock: Meditations on Black Catholic Identity,*[16] uses religious experiences of enslaved African Americans to construct a black Roman Catholic identity. Brown uses the spirituals, created by African American workers who were enslaved, as the primary cultural expressions for Catholic identity. To be authentically black and truly Christian, we have to see the spirituals as cultural creations. Spirituals raise a host of helpful questions: How are they communicated and received? What impact do they have as song, poetry, and dance? What implications can we draw from their rhythm and call-and-response style? For Brown the creation of song is both a religious and a political process.

Afrocentricity

The third category in second-generation black theology draws on a broad 1980s revival in Afrocentricity.[17] Afrocentricity attempts to remove Eurocentric language and practice from the faith and focus of black activities and, as a substitute, position African spirituality, worldview, culture, ideals, and behavior at the very center of all things pertaining to people of African descent. Afrocentricity repositions Africans in America by making them actors in and agents of human history.

For instance, Cain Hope Felder's *Troubling Biblical Waters: Race, Class, and Family*[18] focuses on black people's relation to the Bible and black presence in the Bible. In addition to his scholarly arguments that African Americans bring an African perspective to their use of scriptures, Felder also documents African figures (with their crucial roles and influence) in the Hebrew and Christian Testaments. In fact, Walter Brueggemann, a leading biblical scholar and a past president of the Society of Biblical Literature, stated the following about Felder's work: "We are discovering that what we thought was objective scholarship really turns out to be white scholarship that is very much limited by our cultural categories and cultural horizons."[19] Obviously, Afrocentricity, at least in Judeo-Christian Bible studies, has called into question the dominance of white intellectual categories and interpretations of God's word.

Felder has also edited *Stony the Road We Trod*,[20] a complex and scholarly collection of essays by leading black biblical academics in the United States (a total of ten contributors). All the contributors agree that biblical analysis and interpretation in U.S. churches and intellectual institutions have been Eurocentric. This has meant the absence or marginalization of non-Europeans and blacks in white people's approach to the Bible. The biblical field, the contributors assert, has been dominated by white American males and European academics for several centuries. In contrast, essays in this anthology look at Afrocentricity throughout the entire Bible. One important question that ties the entire collection together is: Where are white people in the Bible? The authors conclude that the Bible is a multicultural document with a heavy presence of African and nonwhite peoples.

Likewise, Robert Hood's *Must God Remain Greek? Afro Cultures and God-Talk*[21] positions Afrocentricity at the heart of theological language. Basically, Hood, a systematic theologian,

questions whether or not Africans and those in the diaspora
have to shed the substance and form of African cultures in order
to claim authentic Christian religious expressions. He also discovers a fundamental role for African presence in the origin and
development of Christianity.

Though not explicitly described as Afrocentric theology,
Hood's final book, *Begrimed and Black: Christian Traditions
on Blacks and Blackness,*[22] does touch on related themes and
concerns. In this work, Hood discovers a basic contradiction
in the definition and symbolism of "blacks and blackness" in
the West and the United States; that is, blacks and blackness
are perceived simultaneously as evil and erotic, and with fear
and fascination. This contradiction (fundamental to the constitution of the West and the United States) grows out of Greek
and Roman heritage and is woven into the Christian tradition.
Moreover, this way of seeing blacks from two opposite opinions constitutes the original myth which, from the perspective
of Hood, determines contemporary race relations to such an
extent that our civil ideal of racial tolerance and inclusiveness
becomes weaker and begins to deteriorate.

In Jon Michael Spencer's *Sing a New Song: Liberating Black
Hymnody,*[23] the reader faces a more open and frontal assault
against Eurocentrism and a bold assertion of Egypt and Africa
as the key to black American faith and witness. Spencer believes that the black church needs a new hymnody because it
is captive to Eurocentric hymns, which are based in Eurocentric
biblical interpretation. The latter, Spencer argues, support sexism, racism, and classism. Indeed, for Spencer, black hymns are
not far removed from the ones learned from white slaveholders
of black Americans and from colonizers of Africa. As an answer, Spencer calls for a look back to African cultures in order
to write a revised black hymnody free from sexism, racism, and
classism.

With Theodore Walker's *Empower the People: Social Ethics
for the African-American Church,*[24] we move from biblical

studies, systematic theology, and theomusicology to the discipline of ethics. Walker draws most explicitly on leading Afrocentric theorists such as Cheikh A. Diop, Ivan Van Sertima, Martin Bernal, and Yosef A. ben-Jochannan. Walker develops a black theological social ethic which accepts the philosophy of black power and is written from an African American churchly perspective. The social ethic offered by Walker involves "breaking bread" — the sharing of the spirit, food, money, land, power, and other resources with the people. By thus empowering the people through bread-breaking, the resurrected Jesus appears within an African framework.

Afrocentricity brings to black theology a unique dimension which instructs the black church and community to base their entire religious and everyday lives on positive African values, beliefs, and practices. In summation, Afrocentricity is a recent attempt to replace Europe with Africa as the core of black religious worship and scholarship. For some African American religious academics and preachers, a cultural future for black Americans must be constructed by letting Egyptian antiquity play the same role that Greek and Roman antiquity serves for Western culture. Afrocentricity, consequently, undertakes a comprehensive project of deconstruction. Afrocentric believers debunk, disentangle, and demythologize the supremacy of Europe as the nucleus of black thought and belief.

Remaking Traditional Disciplines

Black religious scholars of the second generation have struggled to remake traditional disciplines. Their dilemma is "to speak as 'one of the canonical boys' and as 'the noncanonical other' at one and the same time."[25] African American professors are all members of educational institutions and use the language and tools of intellectuals. But, at the same time, they attempt to reform the academy in very creative ways so that these intellectual institutions are more relevant to the larger black environment (e.g., the African American community and churches).

For example, there is a growing body of writers looking at the Bible from a black perspective. These African American biblical teachers use standard skills for interpreting the Bible. But the answers they get from Holy Scripture are different from those white Bible teachers get.

Walter Arthur McCray's two-volume *The Black Presence in the Bible*[26] presents the black and African identities of biblical persons and places and looks into the Table of Nations in Gen. 10:1–32. His emphasis is on using a black vantage point to examine the family and cultural background of Ham. Joseph V. Crockett's *Teaching Scripture from an African-American Perspective*[27] gives four strategies for an African American evaluation of scripture — the story, exile, sanctuary, and exodus approaches. Crockett's focus is scriptural education with cultural integrity. People experience the Bible within their cultures. So when we teach the Bible, we have to be aware of the culture in the Bible and our own culture that we bring when we read the holy word.

Stephen B. Reid's *Experience and Tradition: A Primer in Black Biblical Hermeneutics*[28] asks the following question: What is the connection between black biblical interpretation and black experience? For Reid, the African American identity acts as an organizing factor holding the two aspects together, and the answer about the connection between the two is found in the black church. In addition, by combining biblical interpretation with the black experience, Reid suggests three types of theology. Unity and partnership go with pastoral theology; patriotism and loyalty lead to liturgical theology; and suffering and critical awareness lay the basis for political theology.

Finally, Thomas L. Hoyt Jr.'s *A Study of the Book of Romans: The Church in Your House*[29] establishes the meaning of the book of Romans and its application to today's black family. And with that approach, Hoyt correlates the family of God with the African American family. He calls on Christian believers to live individually and communally as free persons, following the Spirit of Jesus Christ, which, for Hoyt, is the context for everyone's liberation.

In their attempt to bring new insights to the old ways of studying the Hebrew and Christian Scriptures, black biblical scholars have concluded that the Bible condemns every African American household and church that still worships an image of a white Jesus. Moreover, they challenge Christians of all colors in the United States to throw off European male models of Christ and of other biblical figures. At the same time, however, black Bible scholars affirm the centrality of an African American presence in the Bible, black folk's main book of God's word. They also reclaim the many different cultures within scripture, with emphasis on the specific presence of Africans and blacks. The growing tendency among African American Bible scholars is that Christ, like Moses, was an African or black person.

James H. Evans Jr.'s *We Have Been Believers: An African American Systematic Theology*[30] moves carefully through the standard doctrines of black theology and provides an exact definition of black theology and how it relates to the general understanding of systematic theology. He takes traditional Christian dogmas and reworks them. He, in addition, maps out three major tasks for black theologians. (1) Contextual analysis locates any talk and practice with God in concrete histories, cultures, and social, political, and intellectual communities. (2) Critical assessment of the faith of the black believing community brings new life to the faith and makes clear why, what, and how African American believers believe. (3) A constructive black theology must examine the practice of that faith in the world; it investigates the moral implications of Christian belief. Like the first generation of black theologians, Evans supports the historical and persistent realities of faith and freedom in the black church tradition. African American people continue to believe in God's revelation in their struggle for liberation.

Just as biblical scholars and systematic theologians are looking again at the Hebrew and Christian Scriptures from the perspective of African Americans, so too are black ethicists using a similar approach to their traditional disciplines. Robert M. Franklin's *Liberating Visions: Human Fulfillment and Social Justice in African-American Thought* examines Booker T. Washington, Martin Luther King Jr., W. E. B. Du Bois, and Malcolm X because these four men, among other black people, "have developed distinctive and significant traditions of moral thinking and social criticism."[31] Franklin explores each man's particular vision of the just society and human fulfillment and how these ideas impact the entire U.S. society. "Their perspective is essential to a genuine intellectual and social history of the United States."[32] The moral positions and ethical lessons of these four men inform black theology, states Franklin, of the need for personal renewal in order for African American people, and all communities, to be authentically free. Personal and psychological transformation goes along with structural changes in society. Otherwise, black theology and African American churches will fall short of creating a black life of integrity and fulfillment.

Enoch H. Oglesby, in *Born in the Fire: Case Studies in Christian Ethics and Globalization,*[33] expands black liberation ethics to the international arena and remakes further the traditional discipline of ethics. To do black theology of liberation or ethics as true Christians, we ought to recognize and experience different cultures and religious faiths around the world. With his phrase "globalization ethics," Oglesby points to his path toward the correct social relationships among all the earth's peoples. The definition of global ethics means different communities must leave their own context and enter into conversations with people in other contexts. In this unfamiliar dialogue, there exists an inevitable risk of each person's culture being challenged by the other (i.e., dialogue partner) and the Other (i.e., Jesus Christ). Refining his definition, Oglesby asserts:

What, then, is globalization ethics? Globalization ethics is not oriented toward conventional morality, which is based on blind loyalty to traditional creeds and church dogma. Rather, it is based on the revelation of Jesus Christ as the new paradigm for the moral life. Globalization ethics has its own distinctive norms and sources. Its integrative norm is Jesus Christ as Liberator and Reconciler in our broken world.[34]

Moreover, for the church to carry out its world mission of liberation of the poor and the oppressed, Oglesby believes, the Christian faithful must meet certain preconditions: the cultivation of Christian humility, analyzing concrete case studies of faith and liberation, mutual confession in conversation, and naming our suffering as a reminder of God's care and righteousness for us.

From black ethicists, we hear not only the demand for reliance on materials from both the black church and community, but also an insistence that the purpose of all African American religious scholarship is to carry out a practical ethical and moral transformation both of North American structures in society and of individual, personal journeys. Furthermore, in certain instances, the question of what one ought to do in advancing a black liberation ethic connects with global obligations.

Global Connections

Another second-generation trend agrees with a focus on structural domestic evils. However, the writers of this persuasion add the vital importance of linking all black liberation to allies in Africa and its descendants throughout the globe. Following Malcolm's belief that the black folk's struggle in Mississippi cannot be divorced from Africans' movement in the Congo and taking Martin Luther King's saying that we are all interwoven in one inescapable web of destiny, this trend has presented research tying domestic and international efforts of black theology.

Because God has created black beautiful and black people free all across the earth and because European colonialism and slavery and white-skin privileges attempt to push black and African peoples below the realm of human beings, black theology in global connections affirms the divine origin of all African people of the world.

Furthermore, while the second-generation global-connections trend points to a unique relation between black American liberation theology and its distant cousins in Africa and throughout the world, at the same time black theology unites its liberation theology with all of the world's oppressed who struggle within God's purpose of justice on earth. What binds the black liberation theology of African Americans with other peoples of African descent and with theologies of liberation in the Third World are the historical and current consequences of monopoly capitalism.

In other words, the past rise of capitalism and its existence today suggest a fact of capital accumulation by ruling-class families of the globe (primarily based in the United States and Europe) who keep their monopoly over God's resources by taking capital from people of color and the Third World. Injustice against God comes from monopolized capital, which is stolen from blacks, other people of color, and Third World nations. By biblical definition and by definition of the poor's contemporary experience with God, God's earthly justice means each person reaching her or his full individual potential while, at the same time, aiding the well-being of communal relations. To return God's capital and resources back to the poor (i.e., the majority world community) and to reach each person's individuality are the content of God's new community on earth.

Developing a black theology in global connections, Noel L. Erskine's *Decolonizing Theology: A Caribbean Perspective*[35] notes how the problem of identity plagues the Caribbean oppressed peoples because European and North American Christian colonialists and missionary imperialists implanted a foreign God on the islands. In a word, to experience God as imported by European and North American Christian foreigners obscures the true identity and consciousness of the oppressed Caribbean people. The quest for black identity in the Caribbean, therefore, requires a decolonization of a colonized Caribbean theology. So Erskine advocates a black theology of liberation. But liberation, for him, does not go far enough — the goal of liberation is *freedom,* which becomes the true goal of all theologies. In Erskine's words:

> [T]here is a logical step from a consideration of black religion to an articulation of a theology of freedom, because black religion is black people's search in history for freedom. God was for black people the symbol of freedom. So, in the quest for a theology of freedom it becomes appropriate to ask about hope's relationship to freedom.[36]

Kortright Davis's *Emancipation Still Comin': Explorations in Caribbean Emancipatory Theology*[37] argues for emancipation as the core and heart of Caribbean existence. In fact, at the center of the Caribbean experience is a common love for freedom. Closely related to the people's desire for freedom, in particular the poor's desire for liberation historically and today, we find God's purpose aimed at setting the captives free. Thus, emancipation is God's vision for the Caribbean oppressed people. The connection between the marginalized people's struggle for freedom and God's ongoing plan for emancipation provides, for Davis, solid ground for a theology of liberation in the Caribbean. To deepen further and more intentionally a refined Caribbean theology of liberation, Davis details the prospects of emancipation from below (in contrast to one imposed from above by foreign powers or domestic elites).

First, an emancipatory theology of liberation acknowledges liberation theology existing in the history of Caribbean slaves' resistance to slavery. Second, emancipation from below requires healthy ties to other poor people in the rest of the world, especially to the Third World oppressed. Third, we have to affirm creole languages as cultural emancipation and not allow the use of English to denigrate Caribbean indigenous language creations (e.g., the widespread speaking of local dialects in the Caribbean). Fourth, education should center on freedom, and, fifth, race relations should promote harmony and mutuality. Finally, freedom calls for political and economic sovereignty. Beneath all of these human attempts, we meet God's emancipatory work in the past and in possibilities for the future — namely, the promotion of human dignity, renewal of the church, and diverse denominational cooperation.

Josiah U. Young's *Black and African Theologies: Siblings or Distant Cousins?*[38] examines black theology of liberation in the United States (emphasizing a freedom from racist systems) and African theologies (highlighting indigenous cultures) as two processes vital to church integrity. Despite surface tensions and conflicts, both theologies, Young states, have common agreements, but these commonalities are hidden within the context of their differences. Therefore, when we discuss this unity, a basis for a Pan-African theology emerges.

Furthermore, in his *A Pan-African Theology: Providence and the Legacies of the Ancestors*,[39] Young undertakes the development of a Pan-African theology, which he calls for in his first book. The Pan-African theology that he offers draws on the strengths of both sides of the Atlantic, joins a social analysis for the liberation of the African American under class with an analysis of the African peasantry, and, at the same time, embraces black religion and African indigenous religions. With the ancestors showing us God's image, God also reveals God's self in Christ, thus further drawing all African peoples closer to the divine. Following God's plan and armed with a Pan-African consciousness, black theology and African theologies are challenged to work for liberation on earth.

My *Black Theology USA and South Africa: Politics, Culture, and Liberation*[40] represents the first attempt at engaging critically and constructing positively a dialogue between black theologians of liberation in the United States and their counterparts in South Africa. The purpose of the book is to interpret black theology in the United States and black theology in South Africa for a unified agenda. It poses and seeks to answer one major question: What is the common denominator between the two black theologies? It develops one basic claim: both theologies understand political and cultural liberation as the heart of the gospel message. For black Christians in particular and the black community in general, this core message translates into the gospel of political and cultural liberation against racism and other forms of oppression. Finally, the book asserts that several points of agreement exist for a common black theology of liberation across the Atlantic. Among these points are historical-contemporary, theological, normative, and source-basis commonalities. Other areas on which to concentrate are black and African women, black churches, black culture, political thought, and social analysis and vision.

Using a similar approach, Simon S. Maimela and I edited a collection of essays from the first international conference between black theologians in the United States and in South Africa. Titled *We Are One Voice: Essays on Black Theology in the USA and South Africa*,[41] this anthology indicates a distinct focus, that of the black poor. As a result, articles elaborate on the progressive and transformative emphasis in black theology: from black biblical interpretation to the theological significance of black working-class culture to the contributions of women in black theology. The essays in this volume point to the diversity, tensions, and vibrancy of black theology within each country and between both movements.

Drawn together around the gospel mandate to reclaim God's creation of black humanity and to fight white supremacy as sin, both theologies display a growing maturity in relating the complex evils of race, gender, and class against an international backdrop. *We Are One Voice* demonstrates that the black theology of liberation dialogue between South Africa and the United States has built a firm foundation for exploring and sharing contexts, defining common issues, isolating main agenda concerns, and mapping future relations.

George C. L. Cummings's *A Common Journey: Black Theology (USA) and Latin American Liberation Theology*[42] removes the layers of history, doctrines, and future claims of these two liberation theologies and unveils an integral core in the gospel message of freedom. For example, Cummings finds that freedom is part of every aspect of human existence. And theologies of liberation can contribute to constructing a comprehensive theology of the world's poor by consciously connecting to the reality of this emancipation. An inclusive liberation, Cummings believes, arises from American black theology's stress on religion and culture as foundational sources for developing theology and from Latin American liberation theology's focus on social and economic analyses as essential for any form of liberation theology free from bourgeois faith and practice.

In summation, writers within the global connections trend warn black theology in the United States of the dangers of isolation, urging it to stretch forth its hands in partnership with poor people in Africa, the Caribbean, and the Third World.

Challenging Black Theology's Liberation Claim

Black theology of liberation takes for granted the Hebrew Scripture's story about Hebrew slaves achieving liberation with the help of the powerful and nurturing arms of Yahweh. Likewise, the Christian message begins and ends with Jesus' first public sermon regarding freeing the captives and siding with the poor. However, not all black theologians and African American religious scholars want to accept uncritically these theological and theoretical beliefs handed down by first-generation black theologians and quickly embraced by the second generation.

We discover a move to question the Christian claims of liberation in black theology in several books focusing on theodicy and black liberation (i.e., the relation between suffering and freedom). In his work *Why Lord? Suffering and Evil in Black Theology*,[43] Anthony Pinn raises this question: Is the God of Christianity a divinity who supports freedom and liberation? Pinn goes against the black church's long belief in an all-powerful, good, and just God. And he opposes the black church's faith in suffering as redemptive for black positive character, moral leadership, and protest politics. Most African American churches believe that the highest form of this positive suffering is revealed in Jesus' death on the cross at Calvary.

Pinn goes against this African American faith perspective and states that the Christian doctrine of redemptive suffering is flawed and cannot be repaired. Suffering can never be positive or fruitful (i.e., redemptive) for African Americans. Such a faith has been one of the most harmful events in the black history for social transformation because it leads to keeping oppressed African Americans quiet and passive and, on a theological level, exposes God's approval of black people's suffering.

Instead of supporting the black church's belief in the redemptive suffering of Jesus Christ, Pinn calls for a "strong humanism." Because all suffering is bad for blacks and because any God supporting any aspect of suffering as beneficial is, in fact, a harmful God, the freedom of African Americans, for Pinn, will come only from exclusive reliance on black humanity and not from an external being like God or Jesus. It is not God but humans who must fight suffering.

Similarly, David Emmanuel Goatley's *Were You There? God-forsakenness in Slave Religion*[44] seeks to answer how God appears absent from today's intense suffering experienced by African Americans and, secondarily, by the world's poor. After the historic efforts of the 1950s and 1960s civil rights and black

power movements, why does suffering still impact the overwhelming majority of black America? Has God forsaken the
African American community in its current intensified pain?
Goatley answers these questions by drawing on two examples — slavery's cruelty and Jesus' broken body. Even during
slavery, blacks fought, survived, and thrived while maintaining
faith in God.

Likewise, the passion story of Jesus on the cross offers an
educational example of the human-divine exposure to major
pain. Thus to answer the question "Where is God in godforsakenness?" Goatley presents the testimony of enslaved blacks
and the wailing cry of Jesus' crucifixion in Mark 15:34, which
indicates both God's absence and presence for the poor.

Mark L. Chapman's *Christianity on Trial: African-American
Religious Thought before and after Black Power*[45] poses the
following question: Has the black community seen Christianity as supporting oppression or enhancing liberation? Though
this question stems from the African American community's
historical memory of receiving Christianity from a white slave
master and a white Christian preacher (in many instances, both
roles existed in the same person), Chapman concentrates on the
period after World War II — what he calls the pre– and post–
black power eras. Chapman investigates Benjamin E. Mays,
Elijah Muhammad, Albert Cleage, James H. Cone, and Delores
Williams to discover some important criticisms and affirmations
of Christianity's relation to black America.

For example, the pre–black power religious scholars, in
Chapman's estimation, sought integration with white America
and stressed a universal message of Jesus Christ, while their
post–black power counterparts advocated the affirmation of
the black self and the beauty of black particularity. Still, commonalities remain. Both generations, along with non-Christian
thinkers, attacked the racism of white Christian churches and
gave sharp criticisms of the African American church when it
did not serve the poor. And, more recently, black female pas-

tors and scholars have exposed the secondary role of women in the African American church. Chapman thinks we will see the future growth of the black church and its black theology of liberation when they use self-criticism and accept external criticism against all harmful expressions of Christianity.

James Harris's *Pastoral Theology: A Black Church Perspective*[46] does not question the issues of suffering and the positive or negative roles of Christianity. Harris's criticism of black theology states that African American clergy and laypersons are not dealing with issues of black theology of liberation (e.g., the color of God does not interest black people). Therefore, for him, the clergy and laity are out of touch with black theology, and black theologians are out of touch with preachers and the pew. To bridge what he perceives as a gap between the African American church and black theology of liberation, Harris offers the following: respect for black women, increasing tithing, adopting public schools, churches pooling financial resources, surveying the needs of the community around the church, and teaching self-esteem and self-respect.

Criticism and self-criticism indicate a healthy way for a black theology of liberation, in the perspectives of those second-generation theologians who challenge black theology's liberation claim. The lack of structural and ongoing questioning of the main arguments in black theology will leave it stale, dull, and irrelevant to its audience: the African American poor, the black church, and the world's oppressed.

In addition, these theologians challenge black theology at its very core (i.e., its sometimes confident cry of liberation), asking whether its thought and action are really connected with the biblical stories of liberation. Where exactly and how specifically do God, Jesus, and the Holy Spirit carry out liberation? If they do indeed carry out liberation, then why is there suffering for the poor still today, more than two thousand years after the birth of Jesus? What in black tradition and life today shows God, Jesus Christ, and the Holy Spirit working for and siding with the oppressed? What is the relation between black theology of liberation and the everyday Christian black person? And if Christianity is against racism, capitalism, sexism, and heterosexism, then why hasn't Christianity defeated these sins and evils?

Interdisciplinary Studies

A final trend within the second generation is a move toward interdisciplinary studies of black religious thought — the effort to put black theology and black religious scholarship into conversation with bodies of knowledge different from theology. How can black theology relate to sociology, political economy, cultural studies, anthropology, and so on?

Victor Anderson's *Beyond Ontological Blackness: An Essay on African American Religious Criticism*[47] explains why Anderson feels black theology has created an abstract idea of blackness which is not influenced by context, time, and space. There is no one, final idea or identity called "blackness" for all times. Such a static universal totality of blackness denies the cultural fulfillment of different individuals within the African American community. A rule which defines who is really black and who is not will harm people because not all African Americans can fit into such a definition or want to be in it. In contrast, Anderson draws together cultural criticism, postmodern analytical tools, religious criticism, and aspects of anthropological insights to advance his call for black theology to recognize differences within black identity. For Anderson, this identity is constantly changing under the impact of class, gender, and sexual difference.

In addition, in his criticism of the danger of racial consciousness (which he finds in black theology), Anderson states that black theology is simply a reflection of the harmful racial categories of white thought. Indeed, black theology exists because white thought has created it. Whites have created a monolithic black consciousness in black theology, and this abstract, universal identity or idea blocks the ambiguity, difference, and freedom of blacks within the African American group.

The solution, for Anderson, is the cultural fulfillment of each individual within the black community. Such fulfillment would allow an individual black the freedom to choose his or her own marriage partner, move about freely, pursue lesbian and gay goals, and affiliate with different political parties. Anderson denies racial rigidity in black identity and calls for more democracy. Only in this way can each individual black person flourish.

In *Changing Conversations: Religious Reflection and Cultural Analysis*,[48] Sheila Greeve Davaney and I assembled a group of essays bringing black theology and other forms of liberation and progressive theologies in conversation with British and French cultural studies. The contributors to this anthology write from a Christian perspective and discover the divine in concrete cultural contexts influenced by a range of factors. Essays draw on pragmatic historicism, Christian social criticism (informed by political and economic theory), radical philosophy, postmodern insights (from Derrida, Foucault, and Ricoeur, among others), anthropology, popular cultural analysis with its broad range of issues, womanist theological method, black literary criticism, conversations between African theology and South African black theology (supported with cultural and political theories), and a black gay liberation theology grounded in living and dying with AIDS.

And finally, in *Liberation Theologies, Postmodernity, and the Americas*,[49] a core of coeditors and I put black and other liberation theologies in dialogue with postmodernism. Here black theology of liberation enters the conversation with various bodies of knowledge to explore a variety of debates, differences, and common pursuits. From the perspectives of liberation theologies and postmodern theories, this group of essays uses many critical and self-critical areas of study to develop further the project of radical individual and social transformation found in black and other liberation theologies in South, Central, and North America. As the editors state in the introduction:

> Our primary concern in this volume is not to resolve the intriguing intellectual challenges by the meeting between theologies of liberation and postmodernism, but rather to call into question prevailing social systems that refuse to recognize millions of the world's people as human beings. ... Our concern is what this debate [between liberation theologies and postmodernism] means for social strategies that resist domination and advance the full humanity of the powerless.[50]

In addition to the coeditors, other contributors (e.g., Franz J. Hinkelammert, Maria Clara Bingemer, Edmund Arens, Josué A. Sathler, Amós Nascimento, Gustavo Gutiérrez, Elsa Tamez, Jürgen Habermas, Enrique Dussel, Sharon D. Welch, Robert Allen Warrior, and Mark McClain Taylor) examine black and other liberation theologies by using feminist theory, political economy, literary criticism, world history, political theory, legal studies, syncretistic religions, anthropology and sociology, rhetorical studies, and other social and human sciences. Despite its denial of the possibility of ultimate goals and general analysis for all people, postmodernism, the contributors and editors believe, helps because it pushes toward particularity and examines forms of human relationships which are usually different from the dominant traditions. By accepting parts of postmodernism that look at specific communities and marginalized peoples, the Christian project of liberation for the poor, especially in the Americas, can still look for examples of divine emancipation and work toward God's new Common Wealth society on earth.

An example of how second-generation theologians have built new forms of working together is the BT Forum. The original BT Forum consisted of Will Coleman, George C. L. Cummings, James Noel, and myself. The initial gathering took place on the rooftop of Coleman's Berkeley, California, apartment (1988). Without any outside funding, we met once a week for about three and a half years, including semiannual weekend retreats, to discuss the vocation of the African American church and the calling of black theologians. More specifically, we asked: How could African American male scholars maintain a commitment to the poor and working-class communities while teaching in a white environment? The question was about accountability to the gospel of liberation, accountability to the poor black community, accountability to the African American church, and accountability to one's own sanity and soul, while speaking truth to power.

In his summation of the BT Forum, Will Coleman writes:

> The BT Forum represents a tribal style of collaborative co-operation through dialogue, debate, and decision-making that eventuated in several projects, including the writing, with Cheryl Sanders, of *Cut Loose Your Stammering Tongue* (Orbis Books, 1991). This text presents a way of doing theology, especially black theology, that can be effectively executed by young religious scholars who are committed to [a] further redefining [of] theological discourse in the future within a postChristian, postmodern, and pluralistic context.[51]

The BT Forum is an attempt to listen to a calling from God, Jesus, and African and African American ancestors about the necessity to write for and from, as much as possible, the actual words of the poor. In the process, BT Forum members learned from womanists, from other theologians of color, and from the first generation of black liberation theologians. The theme of the forum was "writing our way back home." As Coleman correctly remembers: " 'Home' became a metaphor for our deepest yearning to return (at least through our research and writing) to the psychological, emotional, and spiritual heritage of our African American presence within a predominantly Euro-American environment."[52]

Working Together: Ties between the First and Second Generations

The creative work of the second generation has taken place in conjunction with the founding generation of black theology, which remains both an innovator and an inspiration on several levels. Older African American religious scholars continue to develop and groom black Ph.D. candidates and graduates. This steady production of heirs to black theology's legacy ensures not only the continued publication of African American related texts but also a critical mass of Christian intellectuals who will, in turn, impact the course of theological studies and church leadership well into the twenty-first century. Furthermore, in the doctoral process itself, the seeds of traditions, values, challenges, and novel breakthroughs are nurtured for the entire church, society, and academic institutions. Without these two generations working together, black theology could suffer from a slow hemorrhaging and a certain death.

The BT Forum hosted the first and only meeting specifically called to have a conversation between the first- and second-generation theologians. Over the weekend of April 19–21, 1991, at the Calvin Retreat Center in Griffin, Georgia (just outside Atlanta), black male and female religious scholars began a process of visioning how all generations could work together for the African American church and community.[53] The meeting served as a preliminary discussion on the possibility of formalizing the relation between the first and second generations.

The discussion covered the history of the first generation, its passion for the pain of the poor in the black community, its connection to the African American church, and its ability to work as a group, not as individuals, seeking tenure and promotion in educational institutions. The major points regarding the second generation included the need to deepen the ties with people who sit in the pews of African American churches, to continue training more black Ph.D. students in the discipline of black theology, to address contemporary issues impacting the African American community, to form coalitions with other oppressed groups, to look at the black family and the relation between the black woman and the black man, to help develop local black theology and black religion think tanks and eventually connect them nationally, to collaborate with other disciplines besides theology, and to continue the tradition of radical social analysis.

Basically, the discussion raised the following questions for the second generation: Why is it in the academy? Where is its passion? To whom is it accountable? Is it maintaining the structures of oppression of the black church and community? How can it be for a black theology of liberation when it is a middle-class, professional group sharing privileges with its white colleagues? Has it lost sight of where Jesus Christ the liberator is today? How can scholarly books serve the freedom for the least in society?

A second example of first- and second-generation black theologians working together was the April 2–5, 1998, conference on the thirtieth anniversary of James H. Cone's *Black Theology and Black Power*. Held at the University of Chicago, sponsored by the Martin E. Marty Center at the University of Chicago Divinity School, the Public Religion Project, and the Center for the Study of Race, Politics, and Culture (with cosponsorship from the University of Chicago Campus Ministers and the Rockefeller Chapel), the conference was titled "Black Theology as Public Discourse: From Retrospect to Prospect." As a second-generation theologian and former doctoral student of Cone's, I organized the conference as one way to institutionalize the historical memory of black theology, to pass on the tradition to second- and third-generation theologians, to open up the debate on the current state of the discipline, to lay out some ideas for black theology's future, and to honor the intellectual work of James H. Cone.

All speakers used Cone's *Black Theology and Black Power* (1969) as a critical starting point in their lectures. Church historian Gayraud S. Wilmore (from the Interdenominational Theological Center, Atlanta), political economist Manning Marable (Columbia University, New York City), Rebecca Chopp (provost of Emory University, Atlanta), Rosemary R. Ruether (Garrett-Evangelical Theological Seminary, Evanston, Illinois), social ethicist Emilie M. Townes (St. Paul School of Theology, Kansas City, Missouri — now at Union Theological Seminary, New York City), legal scholar Stephen Carter (Yale Law School), systematic and philosophical theologian David Tracy (University of Chicago Divinity School), Cornel West (Harvard University), and James H. Cone (Union Theological Seminary, New York City) gave major presentations both affirming and challenging black theology today.

The audience included clergy from diverse denominations and racial groups; university and seminary presidents; judges; lawyers; clinical pastoral educators; faculty and students from Chicago area high schools, colleges, and graduate schools; members of the surrounding Hyde Park community and African American communities near the University of Chicago; educators, clergy, students, and media from other parts of the country; federal and state Congress persons; business persons; secretarial staff; laypeople; alumni from the University of Chicago and Union Theological Seminary; and many other representatives of the public (e.g., from the church, educational institutions, and the broader American communities). Parts of the conference were taped by CSPAN.

During the three months leading up to the conference, a group of fifty black high school students in the Chicago area had been holding regular study groups around the reading material on black theology written by conference speakers. In fact, during a break in the sessions, these students held a lively, private question-and-answer and debate meeting with Emilie M. Townes, Cornel West, and James H. Cone.[54] This conference stands as the first major attempt in recent years to make black theology open to the public and to all walks of life.

The First Generation Today

The first generation continues to produce scholarly books that make a difference and that offer theological direction and pace-setting agendas. For instance, James H. Cone's study of Martin Luther King and Malcolm X — *Martin and Malcolm and America: A Dream or a Nightmare*[55] — reflects the mature scholar's pulling together of ten years of investigation and a lifetime of commitment to the least in society. This book is instructive for black theological work because it shows us a new method of producing African American religious scholarship.

Specifically, Cone's ten years of study show how persistent reliance on African American sources yields a new way of doing theology in which everyday black folk can find and learn about themselves. Moreover, Cone has produced a black text which is readable by nonacademic communities (of all races) while it also challenges formally trained scholars to rethink their entire method and content of religious intellectual work. Theology, Cone implies, is real only if it begins outside of universities and graduate schools and reflects the thoughts, metaphors, and ordinary language of people who are not highly specialized. Cone, in this book, places theology further into the public realm of everyday African American life and the broader context of America and the world.

Similarly, C. Eric Lincoln's *The Black Church in the African American Experience* (written with Larry H. Mamiya)[56] concludes a ten-year investigation which updates and changes current interpretations of the black church. It draws on more than eighteen hundred interviews with clergy (rural and urban) and examines the black church in relation to youth, women, economics, politics, music, and more. This groundbreaking text has become the starting point for all serious social-science–based assessments of the state of African American churches.

Several other first-generation scholars continue to publish and add to the growing body of books, thus molding the intellectual growth and faith commitments of the second generation of religious scholars. Gayraud S. Wilmore has edited important contributions to further the academic and popular development of black religious studies. His *African American Religious Studies: An Interdisciplinary Anthology*[57] assembles an impressive gathering of black religious intellectuals in the fields of biblical interpretation, worship, social action, pastoral counseling, theology, and church history to increase the theological education and training of laypersons. And his two edited volumes (*Black Men in Prison: The Response of the African American Church* and *Reclamation of Black Prisoners: A Challenge to the African American Church*) position black Christians and their theology face-to-face with the situation of black prisoners, one of the most neglected areas of the African American community.[58] Finally, Wilmore has updated and revised his classic *Black Religion and Black Radicalism.*[59]

Major J. Jones, in *The Color of God: The Concept of God in Afro-American Thought,*[60] looks again at a basic question about God which was asked in the origin of black theology in the late 1960s. To deal with the color issue, he introduces the idea of "personhood" to unravel the problem and challenge of seeing God as God relates to black persons. Jones believes that part of the agenda of black theology of liberation must still be to free oppressed African Americans from a faith in God colored by alien characteristics. A concept of an alien God can enslave the mind and body of the marginalized black person and deny her or his own true humanity or personhood.

Charles Shelby Rooks's *Revolution in Zion: Reshaping Afri-*

can American Ministry, 1960–1974,[61] looks at the growth
and contributions of the Fund for Theological Education as
it shaped the leadership of black churches of all Protestant
denominations. The fund recruited, maintained, and nurtured
several generations of African American students in their graduate studies for Christian ministries. For nearly twenty-five years,
Rooks stood at the center of this support, and the overwhelming number of Protestant black religious scholars with graduate
degrees today were touched by the fund and Rooks's successful
efforts. His book outlines the history of this process and demonstrates the benefits of a commitment to education and black
religious faith and a practical compassion for justice for sup-
pressed African American voices in the church, academy, and
larger society. How does one identify, sustain, and graduate a
cadre of leadership for the church and black theology? Rooks's
text provides one convincing response.

Vincent Harding's *Martin Luther King: The Inconvenient
Hero*[62] paints a radical picture of King after his famous 1963
"I Have a Dream" speech at the first march on Washington.
Harding attempts to correct the American historical amnesia
about King's last few years before his assassination. At the time
of his Poor People's Campaign scheduled for April 1968 (i.e., the
second march on Washington), King, in Harding's opinion, had
started to condemn U.S. imperialism in Vietnam and other parts
of the Third World. King also held a singular focus on the poor of
all colors, began the prophetic work of a nonviolent revolution
to transform the structures of U.S. capitalism, advocated black is
beautiful, and called for a break with southern conservative and
northern liberal white racism. Harding states that all the plagues
which King fought still confront America today; consequently,
King persists as an inconvenient hero in the contemporary period.

J. Deotis Roberts's *The Prophethood of Black Believers:
An African American Political Theology for Ministry*[63] uses
an ecumenical, cross-cultural, and interdisciplinary method to
elaborate key elements of the black church. Geared toward

both the education of church leadership and increased lay self-awareness, the book touches on education, pastoral care, politics, women, music, faith development, and other aspects of the African American's church ministry. Roberts argues for a black theology linked closely with the black church. Together they become a political theology of protest against white racism and for black liberation.

Peter J. Paris, in his *The Spirituality of African Peoples: The Search for a Common Moral Discourse*,[64] uses his command of religious social ethics and African spirituality to document the continuity of religious and moral values among African peoples. Such continuity, in Paris's study, helps to formulate a theory of moral virtue requiring sorely needed public policies today. Since the ultimate goal of all African peoples is preserving and promoting community, Paris writes, public policies can be shaped to honor the full humanity of each person while the common good is likewise supported. With virtues such as beneficence, forbearance, practical wisdom, improvisation, forgiveness, and justice, America can build a new social contract for the twenty-first century.

Finally, the first generation continues its pacesetting and mentoring role for the second generation of black theologians and African American religious scholars in *Black Theology: A Documentary History, 1966–1979,* and *Black Theology: A Documentary History, 1980–1992*,[65] the two-volume work edited by James H. Cone and Gayraud S. Wilmore. After black theology's beginnings in 1966, no one could answer the question of whether it would soon self-destruct, becoming a mere blip on the radar screen of theological academics and church ministry, or whether it would become a discipline with longevity.

Cone and Wilmore's classic offers a definitive response by presenting the long record of black theology's achievements. Consisting of primary documents from the first *New York Times* open letter to texts on many issues of the second generation, including womanist contributions and works from today's

African American pastor-scholars, these documentary histories present the most comprehensive and representative display of religious scholarship under the broad title of black theology. They testify to the first and second generation struggling together with a self-conscious understanding that God's short-term work with the black and world's poor prepares for a long-term plan for the full humanity of all peoples.

Challenges for the Second Generation

An overall look at the second generation of black theologians today reveals a growth in intellectual interests, sustained work with the first generation, the unique theological contributions of womanist theology, a slow increase in black professors and black students in graduate programs, the deepening of ties between black theology and the African American church (e.g., more second-generation black theologians are pastors and/or work in some capacity with lay members in black churches), and work to strengthen ties with liberation theologies around the world.

The second-generation members face some challenges that are different from those faced by the first generation. For instance, senior scholars had to fight for the right of the African American church and community to think theologically. Prior to the National Committee of Negro Churchmen (1966) and James H. Cone's *Black Theology and Black Power* (1969), the majority white population, which controlled most educational institutions of religion, viewed the notion of a connection between the black church and serious intellectual work as impossible or laughable. Likewise, the civil rights and black power movements were still viewed negatively by the majority of white theologians. As a result, the first generation participated in spirited arguments which led to the birth of all African American religious thought since the late 1960s. The long-term importance of the first generation is that it created black theology and built it as a permanent Christian movement in the United States with influence throughout the world.

Moreover, black theologians had to declare business no longer as usual in predominantly white churches and educational institutions, and they had to teach black churches about their own Christian tradition of struggle and freedom for the oppressed. The first generation of black theologians fought to connect the thinking and practice of all African American people to the message of liberation for the poor in the Bible.

Now the second generation has greater access to support and resources inside and outside religious institutions. The successful work of the first generation has allowed younger scholars to move closer to the mainstream.[66] Consequently, new challenges present themselves. In a word, unlike the older black scholars who primarily fought from outside the mainstream and who were compelled by and related to the life-and-death concerns of a larger societal movement, the second generation finds itself somewhat accepted.

The second generation of black theologians can pursue and fulfill their vocational responsibilities in several ways. First, a crucial thread which should continue to tie together all areas of study and perspectives is a clear focus on the poor. The overwhelming majority in the African American church and community falls within this category. Furthermore, the Christian gospel's emphasis on the bottom of society likewise determines the vocational direction of black theology. Such a pro-poor posture will also sharpen the distinctions between a "black theology of liberation" and a vague "black theology." The former encourages a gospel of good news for all of broken humanity and the radical restructuring of American political economy, while the latter can leave itself open to focus only on reforms. In all of its professional work, the second generation must ask whether it has tried to work for the voices and interests of the African American poor.

A second challenge is to assure that intellectual work remains in service to the church and the community. Intellectual work is a calling from God and is another form of ministry. In the black church, family, and overall community, the complexities of issues in the contemporary period — structural unemployment, AIDS, violence, self-hatred, despair, domestic violence, the existence of one monopoly capitalist superpower, the increasing "feminization of black poverty," examples of positive resistance on the local and national levels, the reality of positive and stable black families and black churches, and so on — demand not less but more rigorous scholarly work.

Furthermore, this academic vocation needs to place liberation theology in conversations at different levels. One audience is the professionals at the undergraduate and graduate levels. A second audience is those engaged in pastoral work — the black clergy situated in the heart of the African American community. And the third and largest audience comprises the masses of black folk — the poor and working class. It is at this level that black theology has to continually remind itself of its audience (i.e., their feelings, pains, goals, fights, language, and hopes). In this sense, the challenge is to speak on three levels with an emphasis on the third audience.

Third, the complexities facing the black community and church in the twenty-first century demand a more sophisticated theoretical framework. What structure of concepts can aid the liberation conclusions and practices of black theology? What insights might be taken from a host of academic disciplines and from actions related to Third World liberation theologies? What theories can help black theology move from its primary sources of the black experience to theological conclusions regarding God's intention for all of oppressed humanity? For example, how does one take interviews with ex-slaves or the rap music of black youth and jump to conclusions about what Jesus Christ is telling poor black folk to say and do? Theory can become a weapon of struggle in the story of God's working with the black poor as they move from being passive victims of oppression to being people actively searching for full humanity.

Fourth, the second generation needs to clearly identify the location of passions of resistance. What are poor people angry about today? For instance, does rap music offer any hints about the state of urban black youths and the (destructive and constructive) potential they offer the black church and community, and, in fact, all of America? Where exactly is the black Christ fighting today beside the broken-hearted and leading a struggle for emancipation? Responses to these questions require the discipline of anthropology and its tools of long-term fieldwork and ethnographic studies of blacks today and tomorrow.

Fifth, the second generation, in order to harness all of its strengths, will have to conduct a prolonged, organized conversation and joint practice between womanists and (male) black theologians. An encouraging model surfaces in *My Sister, My Brother: Womanist and Xodus God-Talk*[67] written by the wife and husband team of Karen and Garth Baker-Fletcher. Their book is a dialogue on God, Christ, humanity, the ancestors, the church, and the last things in Christian hope. A similar model is the ongoing courses titled "Womanist Theology and Black Theology" cotaught by my wife, Linda E. Thomas, and myself. The courses take place at Garrett-Evangelical Theological Seminary (Evanston, Illinois) and the University of Chicago Divinity School. Using the disciplines of anthropology and systematic theology, our specific approach is to put womanist and black theologies in dialogue around issues of race, gender, class, sexual orientation, and ecology.

Finally, the second generation will have to build and evaluate models of basic Christian communities in local areas. Such an effort, whether centered around a particular church or household meetings of African American Christians, would teach, preach, and practice a black theology of liberation for all to see and hear. If there will be third and fourth generations of black theology, then the second generation will have to meet these challenges and more.

Chapter 4

Womanist Theology

The previous chapter examined the diversity and issues confronting the second generation of black male theologians and African American religious scholars. Although they come out of that second generation, womanist theologians and ethicists (e.g., African American women academics and pastors) have charted their own theological journey. They have challenged both the first and second generations of men theologians with issues of faith and practice which go as far back as the origin of black women in America, through the 1960s civil rights movement, up to today's African American church.

Historical Backdrop

When European slave traders brought twenty Africans to Jamestown, Virginia, in August 1619, three of them were women. Here were planted the historical seeds of the plight, the resistance, and the future celebrations of African American women.

For instance, Fannie Lou Hamer, a Christian civil rights activist and a black southern worker in the 1960s, was a direct descendant of enslaved blacks. Born in Mississippi, Hamer was one of twenty children in a sharecropper family living on a white man's plantation. She began picking cotton at age six. Fired because of her civil rights activities, she eventually became a field secretary of the Student Non-violent Coordinating Committee and helped organize the Mississippi Freedom Democratic Party (MFDP). On behalf of the MFDP, Hamer spoke at the 1964 National Democratic Party Convention in Atlantic City, where Lyndon B. Johnson was nominated as the Democratic Party's presidential candidate.

Hamer was black, a woman, a Christian, and from the southern rural working class. She states:

> The special plight and the role of black women is not something that just happened three years ago. We've had a special plight for 350 years [since 1619]....But we are not only going to liberate ourselves. I think it's a responsibility. I think we're special people, [and] God's children are going to help in the survival of this country if it's not too late.[1]

Hamer's Christian views speak to womanist faith and thought about a God of liberation who relates to the particular situation of African American women while, at the same time, being involved in the freedom of all the oppressed. Hamer emphasizes the key of liberation in her struggle when she continues: "We have a job as black women to support whatever is right, and to bring in justice where we've had so much injustice." However, this movement for justice has been especially difficult for black women, even more difficult than for their black men.

From slavery (1619 to 1865) until today, black women have been characterized by negative stereotypes in various ways: Mammy (the devoted, overweight, nonsexual type who supervises other servants and workers), Jezebel (the one with loose morals who sexually tempts all men), the Mule (the one who can work through all sorts of pain and is also made for giving birth to lots of children), and Sapphire (the extremely assertive one with a sassy tongue who dominates and provokes fights with black men because of her pushy nature).

However, in real life, the African American woman has not been like these inhuman stereotypes. She has been and remains a human being with complexities, pain, joy, weaknesses, and strengths like all others. At the same time, her role in American society has been unique. During slavery, she not only did all the jobs that black men performed but also was subject to rape by any type of white man. And she served as a breeder for more slaves for the plantation owner. In fact, white men placed black women in a special category called Breeders. Her sexual worth for the plantation system was seen in a specific role, that of the Fancy Women; those black women, usually the offspring of a white slavemaster and a black female slave, were purchased by white men as sexual ornaments.

Yet these women were not simply objects who quietly accepted the stereotypes or roles in the slavery system. Many resisted by running away, poisoning their masters, participating in group slave revolts, or simply finding ways to prevent pregnancies or slow down the pace of their work schedules. Others developed daily social networks of survival. "The organization of female slave work and social activities not only tended to separate women and men, but it also generated female cooperation and interdependence."[2] They quilted and washed clothes together. They developed their own medical remedies.

And then there were the more well-known heroines like Harriet Tubman, who escaped from slavery and continued to return to lead others on the Underground Railroad, the secret escape route from the south to the north and to Canada. As a Christian freedom fighter, Tubman carried a gun, was nicknamed Moses, and never lost a "passenger" she brought out of the slavery South. Sojourner Truth, in contrast to Tubman, was a former slave and joined the liberation movement while a free person. A black Christian woman, Truth organized tirelessly for the abolition of slavery and for the rights of women. Her famous "Ain't I a Woman?" speech in 1851 at an Akron, Ohio, women's rights convention shows the double race-and-gender leadership provided by African American women.

Today black women still are overwhelmingly workers. In

fact, they hold a triple status in America: as workers, as women, and as members of the black community. To maintain their sense of survival, dignity, and freedom to resist, many African American women have been leaders in black churches, in the black women's club movement, and in the survival and relative independence of the black family. Despite the fact that men control the role of pastors in most African American churches, women remain the financial supporters, dedicated volunteers, and moral pillars of these Christian institutions.

Furthermore, black women stood at the forefront of the civil rights movement. Indeed, Rosa Parks, a black Christian, started the movement when she refused to give her bus seat to a demanding white man in Montgomery, Alabama, in 1955. Similarly, Ella Baker played a decisive (but unrecognized) role in the Southern Christian Leadership Conference, and she also initiated the Student Non-violent Coordinating Committee. Both organizations, along with black churches, proved to be the backbone of the civil rights struggle. And African American women filled the pews of black churches.

Likewise, today black women make up 70 to 80 percent of most black churches. Many of the issues and challenges remain the same; triple discrimination of gender, race, and class confront most African American women. To address this discrimination, black women have developed a spirituality of persistence, creativity, and transforming acts of courage, a spirituality perhaps best summed up in Alice Walker's phrase "in search of our mothers' gardens."[3] Denied senior positions in most black churches, kept in the lower rungs of the job market and professional positions, subject to sexual violation by both white and African American men, and never quite sure about the stability of white women's support, black women have endured like a plant crushed to the earth but never smothered completely. For Christian and other women of faith, this journey into the sunlight has given them strength to rename themselves "womanist."

The Rise of Womanist Theology

"Womanist theology" is the name chosen by black women in various fields of religion who wish to claim two things. First, black female religious scholars, pastors, and laywomen emphasize the positive experiences of African American women as a basis for doing theology and ethics. Black women are made in God's image, and therefore their values, voices, experiences, looks, and ways of being in the world have positive, divine significance.

Second, the title womanist theology calls attention to the negative experiences of black women when they confront both the racism of white feminist and white male theologians and the sexism of black and white male theologians. Womanist theology grows out of black theology and therefore separates its theological claims from white feminist theologians who ignore racism. In this instance, African American female scholars join with their black brothers in the struggle against white supremacy in the church, society, and educational institutions. In other words, the reality of being black in America unites womanist and black theologies.

At the same time, African American women's female experiences in patriarchal America lay a basis for their coalition with white feminists. African American female religious scholars have to live out their dual status of race and gender before God. They cannot separate their reality of being a black person from their reality of being a woman. Both of these experiences go into defining who the African American woman is. To sum up, womanist theology says that there is a unique relation between God and black women, on the one hand. On the other, womanist theology struggles against discrimination caused by white supremacy and by patriarchy.

Womanist theology, moreover, takes its theological guidelines from the definition of womanism given by Alice Walker's 1983 statement in her book *In Search of Our Mothers' Gardens: Womanist Prose:*

Womanist 1. From womanish. (Opp. of "girlish," i.e., frivolous, irresponsible, not serious.) A black feminist or feminist of color. From the black folk expression of mothers to female children, "You acting womanish," i.e., like a woman. Usually referring to outrageous, audacious, courageous, or willful behavior. Wanting to know more and in greater depth than is considered "good" for one. Interested in grown-up doings. Acting grown up. Being grown up. Interchangeable with another black folk expression: "You trying to be grown." Responsible. In charge. Serious.

2. Also: A woman who loves other women, sexually and/or nonsexually. Appreciates and prefers women's culture, women's emotional flexibility (values tears as natural counterbalance of laughter), and women's strength. Sometimes loves individual men, sexually and/or nonsexually. Committed to the survival and wholeness of entire people, male and female. Not a separatist, except periodically, for health. Traditionally universalist, as in: "Mama, why are we brown, pink, and yellow, and our cousins are white, beige, and black?" Ans.: "Well, you know the colored race is just like a flower garden, with every color flower represented." Traditionally capable, as in: "Mama, I'm walking to Canada and I'm taking you and a bunch of other slaves with me." Reply: "It wouldn't be the first time."

3. Loves music. Loves the moon. Loves the Spirit. Loves love and food and roundness. Loves struggle. Loves the Folk. Loves herself. *Regardless.*

4. Womanist is to feminist as purple to lavender.[4]

Walker's four-part definition contains aspects of (1) tradition; (2) community; (3) self, nature, and the Spirit; and (4) criticism of white feminism.

History

Womanist theology emerged both from the 1950s and 1960s black civil rights and black power movements and from the 1970s white feminist movement. As the civil rights struggle picked up momentum, pressure, and limited victories, white feminists began to push more strongly for the passage of the Equal Rights Amendment in the late 1960s and 1970s. The results of the feminist movement, from the perspective of womanists, meant at least two things: (1) the increased presence of white women in various jobs and in seminaries; and (2) the realization by African American women that racism still persisted in the feminist movement. Black women, in short, encountered a racial hierarchy among their white female colleagues.

Similarly, in the civil rights and black power movements, African American women experienced discrimination and sexual and domestic violence from black men. The classic story describes a meeting between Stokely Carmichael, then chairperson of the Student Non-violent Coordinating Committee (SNCC), and some black female members of SNCC during the late 1960s. In this conversation, the black women raised questions about the fair treatment and recognition of women in the student organization. Carmichael's response was that black women's place in the movement was in a "prone" position.[5]

African American men carried this type of oppressive attitude and exploitative practice into seminaries. Just as white women were increasing their numbers in graduate schools of religion, so black men were making inroads. When black women began to slowly enter seminaries, they were faced with African American men's resistance to them receiving ordination and with a denial of black women's calling by God, along with instances of sexual abuse.

The term "womanist theology" came into use after a 1979 article by Jacquelyn Grant which spoke about a black feminist theology. Titled "Black Theology and the Black Woman," the article called into question black theology's fundamental claim — that it is a theology of liberation. The article demonstrated how black theology contradicted its own claims, evidence, warrants, qualifications, and criteria.

Specifically, Grant argued that if black theology described itself as a theology of liberation, meaning that Jesus Christ was with the most oppressed and God was working for the liberation of the least in society, then why was it that black theology was at best silent about black women and at worst oppressing African American women? Grant also drew lines of theological difference with white feminist theologians but stated that the primary focus of her article was the development of a black woman's voice in black theology.

Grant concluded that black women had been invisible in black theology. This was true either because black women had no place in the practice of God-talk and God-walk or black men were capable of speaking for black women. Similar conclusions could be drawn about black women in the African American church and the larger society. Grant wrote the following:

> If the liberation of women is not proclaimed, the church's proclamation cannot be about divine liberation. If the church does not share in the liberation struggle of black women, its liberation struggle is not authentic. If women are oppressed, the church cannot be "a visible manifestation that the gospel is a reality."[6]

In her 1985 article "The Emergence of Black Feminist Consciousness," Katie G. Cannon produced the first written text to use the term "womanist." There she writes:

> Black feminist consciousness may be more accurately identified as Black womanist consciousness, to use Alice Walker's concept and definition. As an interpretive principle, the Black womanist tradition provides the incentive to chip away at oppressive structures, bit by bit. It iden-

tifies those texts that help Black womanists to celebrate and to rename the innumerable incidents of unpredictability in empowering ways. The Black womanist identifies with those biblical characters who hold on to life in the face of formidable oppression. Often compelled to act or to refrain from acting in accordance with the powers and principalities of the external world, Black womanists search the Scriptures to learn how to dispel the threat of death in order to seize the present life.[7]

Cannon's scholarship introduced womanism as the innovative and new category for all black women's religious work. However, the first text using the specific term "womanist theology" was Delores S. Williams's article "Womanist Theology: Black Women's Voices," which appeared in the March 2, 1987, edition of *Christianity and Crisis*.[8] In that piece, Williams uses Alice Walker's definition of womanism as a theoretical outline to sketch a black women's theology.

Further defining the quiltlike configuration of womanist diversity in harmony and solidarity, Linda E. Thomas writes the following about the complementing threads and rainbow mixtures in womanist theology:

We are university, seminary and divinity school professors. We are ordained and lay women in all the Christian denominations. Some of us are full time pastors; some are both pastor and professor. We are preachers and prayer warriors. We are mothers, partners, lovers, wives, sisters, daughters, aunts, nieces and we comprise two thirds of the black church in America. We are the black church. The church would be bankrupt without us and the church would shut down without us. We are from working class as well as middle class backgrounds. We are charcoal black to high yellow women. We love our bodies; we touch our bodies; we like to be touched; we claim our created beauty. And we know that what our minds forget our bodies remember. The body is central to our being. The history of the African American ordeal of pain and pleasure is inscribed in our bodies.[9]

Method

In the development of theology and ethics, womanists write about a total relation to God (i.e., a holistic relationship). They believe in the positive sacred-human connections at the locations of gender, race, class, sexual orientation, and, to a certain degree, ecology. In fact, a holistic methodology and a holistic worldview constitute what it means to do womanist theology. Womanist theology is holistic in terms of (1) the many theological ways black women face oppression and·struggle for liberation; (2) the use of many disciplines of analyses; and (3) the diverse dimensions of what it means to be a human being — that is, the spiritual, cultural, political, economic, linguistic, aesthetic, and so on. Furthermore, from the perspective of Delores S. Williams, womanist theological method is

> informed by at least four elements: (1) a multidialogical intent, (2) a liturgical intent, (3) a didactic intent, and (4) a commitment both to reason and to the validity of female imagery and metaphorical language in the construction of theological statements.[10]

Multidialogical intent allows Christian womanists to engage in many conversations with different people from various religious, political, and social communities. The desire of womanists in these exchanges is to focus on the "slow genocide" of poor African American women, children, and men caused by systems of exploitation. Liturgical intent means that black female religious scholars and clergywomen will develop a theology relevant to the African American church, especially its worship, action, and thought. At the same time, womanist theology challenges the black church with the prophetic and critical messages coming from the practice of black women. In a word, black church liturgy has to be defined by justice.

Didactic intent points to the teaching moment in the theology of the black church as it deals with a moral life determined by justice, survival, and quality-of-life ethics. All of these concerns commit us to a language which is both rich in imagination and reason and filled with female stories, metaphors, and imagery.

Part of the methodology of womanist theology includes both epistemology and practice, that is to say, how we obtain knowledge and how we witness in ethics. How do womanists get their knowledge, and how does knowledge relate to their practice?

In the analysis of Kelly Brown Douglas, womanist theology is accountable to ordinary women — poor and working-class black women.[11] This means three things: (1) Womanists must teach beyond the seminaries and divinity schools and go to churches and community-based organizations to learn. Put differently, "it will be church and community-based women who will teach womanist theologians how to make theology more accessible."[12] (2) If womanist theology is to be accountable to church- and community-based women, then womanist conversations must take place beyond the academy. Womanist theology must have as its primary talking partners and primary location poor and working-class women in their families, churches, and community organizations. (3) Womanist theology must work with church women to help empower them and to help them speak their voice so that church leadership will respond or change. As noted earlier, black women constitute 70 to 80 percent of most African American churches and are the financial supporters and workers of the church.

Moreover, for Linda E. Thomas, womanist methodology "validates the past lives of enslaved African women by remembering, affirming, and glorifying their contributions." After digging up and reflecting critically on the foundational stories of these foremothers, the next step in the methodology is to construct a new model. She writes:

We who are womanists concoct something new that makes
sense for how we are living in complex gender, racial,
and class social configurations. We learn from the rituals
and techniques which our foremothers originated to survive in hostile environments and from how they launched
new perspectives, reconstructing knowledge of a liberative
approach for black women's lives. This self-constituting
dynamic is a polyvalent, multi-vocal weaving of the folk
culture of African American women.[13]

Furthermore, womanist methodology uses ethnographic approaches which allow black women scholars to enter the actual
communities of poor black women "in order to discover pieces
to create a narrative for the present and the future."[14]

Summing up the holistic dimension of the different sources in
womanist theology, Emilie M. Townes states:

Yet the anchor for womanist thought is the African-
American church and its people. The history of the Black
church is not only religious, it is social. The social conditions and worldviews of its people have had an intricate
connection. Womanist thought reflects some of this inti-
macy. Examples of this can be found in the deeply spiritual
and moral aspects [of sacred and secular black writers and
singers]. West African religions, vodun, and folktales are
mediums. Life in the church — from preacher's admoni-
tions to choir crescendos to board meetings and power
struggles — all are resources and guardians of communal
memory and accountability. Academic theological discourse
is also a part of womanist reflection and thought. Such are
the touchstones for womanist reflection.[15]

One of the most creative models for practicing womanist
theological method was initiated by Teresa L. Fry.[16] Over a period of six years, Fry worked with black women in churches,
individual interest groups, and various other organizations.

Membership in the groups she worked with ranged from five hundred to six hundred women. Fry states that the women created S.W.E.E.T. (Sisters Working Encouraging Empowering Together), which was an intentional womanist effort to support black women's attempts at both spiritual and social liberation. The project was truly holistic: the women involved ranged from age seven to seventy-eight; educational levels started at grade school and reached graduate levels; women were married, widowed, single, and divorced; the group included heterosexuals, lesbians, and bisexuals; faith perspectives were ecumenical and interfaith, and some women were unchurched; some "had been incarcerated, [were] on the way to jail or knew someone there"; there were "Deltas, Alphas, Zetas, Sigmas, and Links sitting alongside Granny, MaDear, Mama, Big Momma, and Auntie." S.W.E.E.T. organized

> annual seminars, inclusive seminars, intensive women centered Bible studies, monthly workshops, relationship building exercises, small group discussions, potluck dinners, informal and formal luncheons, community action projects, intergenerational mentoring groups, individual and group counseling sessions, guest speakers, and in group speakers, panel discussions, role playing, ethnographies, health support groups, and African American women's literature study and discussion groups. Alice Walker's definition of womanist was used as the point of departure of each discussion.

The following addition was added to Walker's definition: a womanist also "believes in Somebody bigger than you and me" or "possesses a radical faith in a higher power." Throughout the various sessions, women were encouraged to think for themselves and form their own opinions and models of life by starting with their own stories; each person had a chance to lead meetings. One rule governed all of S.W.E.E.T.'s activities: "We will respect our sisters' space, speech, issues, voice, pain and sensitivities." Women used titles such as Sister and Girlfriend or first names, and elders were respected with the names Mother (for the spiritual anchors of the group) or Miss. Fry's report indicates that the spirituality of the organization was itself holistic, entailing organized Christian beliefs to personalized feelings of the spiritual:

> Women were not pressured to be a member of a church and there was an understanding that the group was spiritually based. Each sister determined and articulated her own sense of spirituality. African American spirituality is the conscious awareness of God, self, and others in the total response to Black life and culture. It is the expressive style, mode of contemplating God, prayer life, and that which nourishes, strengthens, and sustains the whole person. We coupled prayer, testimony, tears, laughter, or silence with embracing each other.

Further activities of S.W.E.E.T. included interviews with and studies about members' mothers, grandmothers, and other mothers; investigations of black women leaders in different fields and in history; discussions on how to change and save the black family based on African family values; black clergywomen in the pulpit, re-visioning liturgies, and seeing women's roles in the Bible; "back to the kitchen table" programs held on Saturday mornings in different homes; an intergenerational group, "It Takes an Entire Village to Raise a Child"; and "loving and care for yourself" gatherings (e.g., concerning hysterectomy, breast cancer, divorce, new Christians, single mothers, exercising, and self-affirmation).

Intellectual Developments

The writing of books on womanist theology is slowly gaining momentum. *Black Womanist Ethics,* by Katie G. Cannon, a graduate of Union Theological Seminary (New York City) in ethics, was the first womanist text to be published. In this work, Cannon sets out to establish womanist liberation ethics. Cannon shows that

> Black women live out a moral wisdom in their real-lived context that does not appeal to the fixed rules or absolute principles of the white-oriented, male structured society. Black women's analysis and appraisal of what is right or wrong and good or bad develops out of the various coping mechanisms related to the conditions of their own cultural circumstances. In the face of this, Black women have justly regarded survival against tyrannical systems of triple oppression as a true sphere of moral life.[17]

However, this moral wisdom does not completely save African American women from institutionalized social evils; rather, it uncovers whatever negative ethics might undermine or attack black women's womanhood. Cannon wants to educate black women about their moral struggle by using the experience of common people as well as the oral tradition. For specific sources, she draws on her own family stories, slave narratives, black folk culture, biblical interpretations, black church history, and the African American women's literary tradition, which, she argues, is "the best available literary repository for understanding the ethical values Black women have created and cultivated in their participation in this society."[18]

From a liberation perspective, she wants to increase the literature on ethics which shows working and poor African American women as moral agents. She uses the disciplines of ethics, history, political economy, and literary studies in a systemic analysis of sex, race, and class. Her aim is to map out survival strategies and a call for action.[19]

Her map has four main components: (1) Canon creates new educational styles based on womanist experiences and knowledge. These styles help to teach students how to be critical in their thinking and be suspicious of the dominant educational system. (2) She develops a new way of looking at social relations between men and women and between whites and blacks. This approach unmasks race, class, and gender oppressions found in structures with hierarchies. Once the oppressions are unmasked, we can then move toward transformation. (3) She criticizes any type of ethics that says that the correct standard is based on European or white American males and how they do ethics, especially how they create theories, debates, and doctrines. (4) With womanist experiences as the judge, Cannon creates "fresh ethical controversies relevant to [black women's] particular existential realities as they are recorded in the writings of African American women."[20]

Cannon works with the established structures within the discipline of ethics, but not uncritically. Indeed, these structures are approached with new questions coming from poor black women's lives. Working within the discipline of history, she discovers the historical context in which African American women have found themselves as moral agents. This history shows patterns of moral wisdom and ethical behavior.

From the perspective of the discipline of political economy, she takes the following stand: "[Once] chattel slavery and White supremacy have become interstructured through capitalist political economy only the elimination of a capitalist mode of production can open the way to making racism dysfunctional."[21] Finally, Cannon shows how the discipline of literary criticism can investigate black women's writings to elicit modes for expressing black women's issues, theological feelings, and ethical conduct.

In the same year that Cannon published *Black Womanist Ethics* (1988), Renita J. Weems published *Just a Sister Away: A Womanist Vision of Women's Relationships in the Bible.*[22] Weems, trained in the Hebrew Bible at Princeton Theological Seminary, uses this work to look beneath the obvious in the Bible to discover a place for women, especially black women, in

God's new community for humanity. For her, an important way of understanding how women see themselves is by investigating how they treat other women. Female relations, consequently, occupy a central role in this text.

Furthermore, part of her method, Weems states, is to examine biblical stories and, out of that reading, create what might have been the possible feelings and concerns of ancient women. She admits that her creative reconstructions make no claim to fact; still, they suggest realistic scriptural testimonies. Her womanist imagination sheds new light on women in scripture. Similarly, her personal commentary unites biblical times with women's struggles today.

Using the story of the Egyptian Hagar and Hebrew Sarai, Weems interweaves themes of social rivalry, sexual abuse, economic exploitation, slavery, and ethnic prejudice. The Genesis story serves as a discussion point for North American black and white women's relations during slavery and even today. Despite the various levels of difference between Hagar (the slave) and Sarai (the slave mistress), Weems concludes:

> At some time in all our lives, whether we are black or white, we are all Hagar's daughter. When our backs are against a wall; when we feel abandoned, abused, betrayed, and banished; when we find ourselves in need of another woman's help (a friend, neighbor, colleague, relative, stranger, another man's wife); we, like Hagar, are in need of a woman who will "sister" us, not exploit us.[23]

The Hebrew Scripture tale about Ruth and Naomi becomes, for Weems, a model expressing profound friendship between a widow and her grieving mother-in-law. Such a special and unique female bonding, furthermore, details a precious friendship which goes beyond nationality, religion, and age differences. Here too the reader discovers the binding commitment between two women who pursue a very rough life without being attached to or defined by males. This is a story of stubborn loyalty and lasting love. As Weems notes: "This is the first commandment of friendship: to be a sister to a friend even when she is neither in a position nor disposition to reciprocate the sisterhood."[24]

In the tale of Queen Esther, Weems imagines the responsibilities and pressures of women married to public figures — that is, the delicate balance between obedience under the public eye and the self-convictions of independent women. In another biblical story (this time concerning friction between Miriam [Moses' sister] and the Ethiopian woman Moses married), Weems investigates the difficult challenge of rivalry against one's sister-in-law and the harmful effects of insecurity and jealousy, both obstacles to women pooling resources for their mutual benefit.

In her *Battered Love: Marriage, Sex, and Violence in the Hebrew Prophets*, Weems focuses on the theme of "sexual violence as a poetic portrayal of divine retribution."[25] She explores the question of how sexuality is imagined and used in the biblical language — for instance, the recurring image of comparing Israel's social and political situation with the experiences of promiscuous women. Furthermore, writes Weems:

> Commentators frequently note the ways in which elaborate descriptions of naked, battered women's bodies function in the prophecies of Hosea, Jeremiah, and Ezekiel as a poetic device for discussing divine punishment and social anarchy. Inveighing, as prophets normally did, against the official practices of the religious and political establishments, all three used imagery associated with bodily functions, particularly those related to female sexuality, to denounce public policies they thought profane and perilous.[26]

Weems explores why the men prophets used for their male audiences such symbols as the promiscuous wife, the mutilated lover, and the aggressive whore. Weems concludes that by associating the issues of marriage and sex with violence, the prophets increased the public's emotions of shame, terror, disgust, and dread. In a related manner, prophetic language united romance and violence, thus causing feelings of fascination and repulsion. In a word, from Weems's perspective, the authenticity of a prophet depended on his ability to link female sexual behavior to God's demands against Israel.

After Cannon and Weems, Jacquelyn Grant published her *White Women's Christ and Black Women's Jesus: Feminist Christology and Womanist Response,* which explores the key idea in the black church, that of Jesus the Anointed One.[27] A graduate of Union Theological Seminary, New York City, Grant trained in systematic theology.

For Grant, African American women experience a three-dimensional reality of sin — racism, sexism, and classism — and therefore must apply a holistic approach in the doing of Christian theology. Racial discrimination and sexist oppression have created a disproportionate number of black women within the ranks of poor and working-class people. Consequently, the everyday survival attempts and resistance struggles of poor black women should anchor and judge the truth of any womanist beliefs.

As a systematic theologian, Grant poses the question, Where do God and humanity meet each other? For her, the answer is that divine revelation comes in two ways to poor black women. First, God makes God's self known by direct communication to poor African American women. Second, God's revelation appears in the Bible; however, black women have to receive and interpret the Bible in their own context. As a Christian systematic theologian, Grant takes seriously the decisive revelatory appearance of God in the black woman's Jesus.

Poor black women, in their everyday lives, have affirmed Jesus in several ways. First, Jesus has been a divine cosufferer who has given them power in times of intense oppression. A process of mutual identification took place in which both Jesus

and poor African American women shared in each other's suffering and empowerment. Second, poor black women called on
the name of Jesus as a way to condemn the demonic earthly
authority-claims of white racists. For these women, because
Jesus was actually God, no human being or race could assert
any claim to divine authority and supremacy. The literal sacredness of Jesus meant that black women did not need to obey or
submit to white people.

Third, both Jesus and poor African American women represent the particular and the universal. Black women (due to their
three-part oppression of gender, race, and class) relate to the
racial suffering of black men, the gender discrimination against
all women, and the economic exploitation endured by all
working-class and poor people. As a result, the tri-dimensional
aspect of black women's oppression not only applies to their
particular situation but also covers the experiences of the
majority of peoples throughout the globe. "Likewise," Grant
writes,

> with Jesus Christ, there was an implied universality which
> made him identify with others — the poor, the woman,
> the stranger.... [F]irst he identifies with the "little people,"
> Black women, where they are; secondly, he affirms the
> basic humanity of these, "the least"; and thirdly, he in-
> spires active hope in the struggle for resurrected, liberated
> existence.[28]

Fourth, Grant describes the idea of Jesus as a theological symbol for poor black women. Symbols are important in
Grant's theology. According to her, a direct connection exists
between theological symbolism and the oppression of women,
especially concerning the use of Jesus' maleness to oppress
women. Yet Grant does not pursue the road of changing Jesus
from a man to a woman. Her conclusion is different. "I would
argue," she states, "that the significance of Christ is not his
maleness but his humanity.... [F]or me, it means today, this

Christ, found in the experiences of Black women, is a Black woman."[29]

Summarizing Grant's approach to the connection between Jesus and black women, we can find at least five characteristics of Jesus which kept African American women sane and encouraged them to keep going daily. Jesus acted as cosufferer (i.e., God in Jesus came to suffer with the poor); equalizer (i.e., because Jesus came for all, Jesus equalizes all); initiator of freedom (i.e., the issue is not just to become equal to an oppressor but to be free); sustainer (i.e., Jesus functioned as family); and liberator (i.e., Jesus' liberation activities gave power to poor black women in their struggle for their own liberation).

Yet, continues Grant, by imprisoning Jesus in male supremacy, white supremacy, and the privileged class, white oppressors have opposed the faith stance and truth beliefs of poor African American women.[30] Male oppressors of women have intentionally used Jesus' male gender to maintain men's hierarchy and dominance in the church and society. This fact, for Grant, stands out in the entire course of Christian history. Throughout Christian history, male oppressors have used the following argument: because Jesus was a male, men are entitled to dominance and control over females. Still, African American women face more than sexism. Racism, observes Grant, has often been seen as the defining characteristic of the black American women's position. In both white and black churches, we find white supremacy lodged systemically in the ongoing use of a white, male, European model to portray Jesus. The Christian church in North America, Grant proclaims, has been a bastion of the sin of racism.

Jesus has been imprisoned not only by sexism and racism but also by the privileged classes in their manipulation of the notion of servanthood. For the rich elite, the idea of servanthood has reinforced the subservience, obedience, and docility of politically oppressed classes and people. The privileged deny the existence of Jesus' real servanthood by changing his poor status into a royal one. Jesus' birth in a stable, his being a Jew, and his death as a common criminal disappear in the theology of the ruling elites. We can sum up Grant's view of Jesus and poor black women with her statement:

> I am arguing that our servanthood language existentially functions as a deceptive tactic for keeping complacent non-dominant culture peoples and the non-privileged of the dominant culture. Thus, the White Jesus, the Jesus of the dominant culture, escapes the real tragedy of servant-hood, but oppressed peoples do not.[31]

Trained in theology at Union Theological Seminary, New York City, Delores S. Williams published her first book, *Sisters in the Wilderness: The Challenge of Womanist God-Talk,* in 1993.[32] Instead of the exodus model supported by black theologians and most womanist religious scholars, Williams inserts provocatively the wilderness imagery as most representative of American black women's reality. Therefore, instead of believing in liberation as the key, Williams states that survival and productive quality of life represent the central thread in womanist theology and ethics (i.e., these are the areas of study and practices which focus on the well-being of all black people — women, men, and children).

Specifically, the Hagar and wilderness concepts gave Williams a biblically based Christian model which deemphasized the authority of males and lifted up the roles of women. Even more, Williams found the Hagar story deeply entrenched in African American traditions and, simultaneously, paralleling black women's experiences today. Instead of God being a liberating divinity, God operated as a supreme being offering survival and hope for a productive quality of life for the African slave Hagar and her son Ishmael. Williams declares:

> I concluded, then, that the female-centered tradition of African-American biblical appropriation could be named

the survival/quality-of-life tradition of African-American biblical appropriation....In black consciousness, God's response of survival and quality of life to Hagar is God's response of survival and quality of life to African-American women and mothers of slave descent struggling to sustain their families with God's help.[33]

Equipped with her new model, in contrast to the central claims of black theology of liberation, Williams rereads the Hagar passage and gives us key social, personal, and religious issues relevant to the survival and quality of life of black women: concerns such as motherhood (a problem within the black community's self-understanding); surrogacy (found both in the pre– and post–Civil War periods); ethnicity (centered on the consequences of skin color); and wilderness (paralleling African American women's and Hagar's life in the wild). A theological exploration of these concerns then leads to a critical conversation with black liberation theology (over method, doctrine, and ethics) and feminist theologies (accenting commonalities and differences among all women of color and white women).

It is in conversation with black theology of liberation that Williams suggests that there is nothing divine in the blood of the cross and Jesus' death. On the contrary, what happened to Jesus on the cross represents human defilement and attack on the divine. Black women should avoid ideas like surrogacy and, instead, cling to the ministerial vision which God gave Jesus when Jesus was alive. Such a ministerial vision of life includes right relationships on earth brought about through words, touch, and kicking out earthly examples of evil. Prayer, compassion, faith, and love would replace these manifestations of evil.

Finally, Williams concludes her analysis with an exposure of the sins the African American denominational churches have committed against black women. Then the remainder of her book poses a hopeful example of a womanist church, as shown in the workings of the Universal Hagar's Spiritual Churches. Though strong male-centered tendencies persist within these churches, which are found throughout the United States, Williams nonetheless sees positive countertrends, highlighting the role of women in theology, ritual, and church administration.

Emilie M. Townes's first book, *Womanist Justice, Womanist Hope*, was likewise published in 1993.[34] Receiving her D.Min. (from the University of Chicago Divinity School) and her Ph.D. in Religion and Society and Personality (from Garrett-Evangelical Theological Seminary), Townes uses Ida B. Wells-Barnett (a late nineteenth-century activist intellectual) for what Townes envisions "as a substantial scholarly historical and ethical inquiry into the social and moral lives of African-American women in the contemporary church."[35] Wells-Barnett serves as an adequate role model for the recovery of black women's tradition because of her strong commitments to both the church and justice. Especially appealing for Townes is Wells-Barnett's social and moral viewpoints, which provide foundational planks for a womanist ethic of justice.

Specifically, Wells-Barnett's social and moral perspectives give us the ingredients for several aspects of a womanist Christian social ethic today. First, the ethic of authority divides into two types of moral practices. One thrives on subjugation and domination while the other more healthy model "reflects community, partnership, and justice." Second, obedience as an additional ethic should avoid the power imbalance between the self over the other or the other over the self, a relationship of blind submission. An appropriate way of obedience figures out the will of God and links justice to transforming the world.

Third, an ethic of suffering is one whose goal is to fight against the reality of suffering. This womanist practice flows from seeing suffering as contrary to God's plan for redemption. In addition, suffering places the victim in a reactive mode which obstructs the need for proactive personal and systemic measures against the causes of suffering.

Fourth, a liberation ethic from a womanist stance sees the spiritual dimension of liberation including pride and self-worth. The spiritual part goes with the social aspect of liberation. When we have both together, then each individual can participate in the world as a proactive social agent. Fifth, a reconciliation ethic acknowledges an objective side where God, through love and grace, has created new social interactions among human beings. The subjective realm becomes real when human beings act to reconcile among themselves in a harmonious fashion.

In her second text, *In a Blaze of Glory: Womanist Spirituality as Social Witness,*[36] Townes sees womanist spirituality emerging out of three black women novelists. Toni Morrison's *Beloved* speaks to black people's very being and survival. Alice Walker's *The Color Purple* shows the context for the cultural images of black women by discovering the different parts of creation and the need for social activism. Paule Marshall's *Praisesong for the Widow* reveals a spirituality linked to self-worth, images of blackness, and self-esteem issues. In sum, womanist spirituality is "embodied, personal, communal," and it is "the working out of what it means for each of us to seek compassion, justice, worship, and devotion in our witness."[37]

Furthermore, Townes has edited two important anthologies which bring together some of the most creative representatives of womanist theology and ethics. The first volume, *A Troubling in My Soul: Womanist Perspectives on Evil and Suffering,* uses various disciplines to try to figure out why African American women experience so much suffering. It is Job's question, "Why Lord?" With the second and companion volume, *Embracing the Spirit: Womanist Perspectives on Hope, Salvation, and Transformation,* we find that trouble does not have the last word. The essays in both volumes are organized under different parts of Alice Walker's definition of womanism.[38]

The Black Christ (1994), by Kelly Brown Douglas, explores the historical and contemporary issues surrounding the African American community's gravitation to a black Christ and then offers a theological response to the question of the color of Christ. Brown Douglas, a systematic theologian trained at Union Theological Seminary, New York City, asks black churches why their focus on the black Christ has empowered them to fight against racism but has left them on the sidelines in the struggle against sexual, class, and gender oppression. The churches, Brown Douglas claims, have failed to keep in balance both Christ's prophetic actions (i.e., commitment to the poor) and his color appearance (i.e., skin pigmentation). Fundamentally, the answer to the question of Christ's color is found in a theological response, and Brown Douglas presents one womanist interpretation.

To give evidence for her argument, Brown Douglas explores a historical context of the perception of the black Christ in the African American community. This perception, for her, sprang from enslaved black people's portrayal of God, black nationalists' usage of the symbol of the black Christ, and black literature's creation of the Christ picture. The American slavery period presented two perspectives on Christ. The slave owners preached a spiritualized white Christ in order to justify the privileges of white skin over black skin. Blacks, in contrast, believed in the prophetic and liberating activities of Christ's daily ministry with the poor and marginalized. Here with the least in slave society, Christ became "a fellow sufferer, a confidant, a provider, and a liberator,"[39] all aspects of a black focus on Jesus' ministry, not on Jesus' abstract spirit.

At the same time, Jesus' ministry helped the enslaved black Christians to wage resistance against Christian white supremacy, in the material and the spiritual world, on earth and in heaven. The presence of Jesus meant the divine gift of God's freedom to enslaved black people, and, thus, the poor and the enchained accepted such a gift by organizing for liberation. It is the enslaved black Christian's focus on Jesus' earthly ministry, a prophetic proclamation and a transformative witness, which defines the black Christ during slavery.

If African American Christians under slavery supported the
critical importance of Jesus' earthly ministry, black nationalists
have identified radically with the black skin color of Christ. At
stake is the self-esteem of blacks and the literal interpretation
of God's image. That is to say, if African Americans are made
in God's image, then God is ebony. Similarly, early twentieth-
century black novels and short stories written by such notables
as Langston Hughes, Countee Cullen, and John Henrik Clark
linked Christ with actual black skin color.

But, in Brown Douglas's reading, in each moment of this historical context (of slavery, nationalism, and literature), no one
comprehensively tied blackness and Christ's liberating activity.
The womanist approach to Christ moves closer in the direction
of such comprehensiveness.

Such a womanist voice, for Brown Douglas, argues for two
main points: one sociopolitical and the other religio-cultural.
A sociopolitical strand speaks to wholeness for the black community:

> Black women have been traditionally concerned, not just
> for their welfare, but for the welfare of their entire com-
> munity and families — sons and daughters, husbands and
> brothers. . . . As a result of their consistent commitment to
> their families and their community, Black women have
> searched for a "politics" of wholeness as they have eval-
> uated their participation in various freedom movements,
> such as the contemporary woman's movement and the
> 1960s Black freedom struggle.[40]

This sociopolitical analysis of wholeness, moreover, highlights
race, gender, class, and sexual oppression as dangers to the well-
being of the entire African American community, but especially
to black women. And this analysis has two sides because it
looks both inside and outside the black community to see how
these harmful practices prevent the full humanity of African

American women and the whole black community and black family.

The other part of the womanist theological voice, for Brown Douglas, is a religio-cultural analysis which embraces the liberating aspects of black religion and culture, not the negative parts. Not everything black or African is healthy for the black community, she argues.

Finally, Brown Douglas claims Christ is black because Christ does have black skin and black features. Further, Christ is black because we meet God as a sustainer, a liberator, and, very important for Brown Douglas, a prophet engaging and challenging the African American community. Finally, with her specific womanist contribution, Brown Douglas states that Christ is found in the faces of the poorest black women in the African American family and community. She confesses:

> I affirm that Christ is found where Black people, men as well as women, are struggling to bring the entire Black community to wholeness. While my womanist perspective highlights the significance of Christ found in the faces of Black women in struggle, especially poor Black women, it does not eliminate the possibility of Christ being seen in the faces of Black men who struggle for Black women's and men's lives and wholeness.[41]

Living with the poorest of the poor and focused on a goal of full life and wholeness, the black Christ is a black woman, but not exclusively.

Karen Baker-Fletcher, with a doctorate in theology from Harvard University, uses Anna Julia Cooper (a late nineteenth-century activist intellectual) as a primary source for developing contemporary womanist reflections. Her *A Singing Something: Womanist Reflections on Anna Julia Cooper* (1994) uses the symbol of voice to discover womanist lessons for today. She writes:

The theme of voice is central to my discussion. I examine Cooper's argument for women's movement from silence and subjugation to a model of bold vocalization and independence to consider how her concept of woman's voice provides a resource for a contemporary theological concept of women's embodiment and prophetic message of freedom and equality. Today, as womanists both build on and move beyond Cooper's thought, we will find it necessary to consider a diversity of women's voices among Black women.[42]

To bring black women's voice to full richness, in Baker-Fletcher's opinion, womanists must take seriously the importance of story, including women's sociological studies, fiction, autobiographies, scholarly essays, discussions with friends, poetry, and song. Out of the story style and the instructive lessons from the life and writings of Cooper, Baker-Fletcher emphasizes five theological themes for womanist theology: the power of voice, the power of making do, the power of memory, the power of holding things together, and the power of generation. These are all God-given gifts found in, but not limited to, African American women who, through their use, have produced survival and an abundant life for black women and their families and communities.

Marcia Y. Riggs received her doctorate in ethics from Vanderbilt University, and her first text, *Awake, Arise, and Act: A Womanist Call for Black Liberation* (1994), "analyzes the moral dilemma that social stratification in the black community poses for black liberation and the ethical praxis needed to address that dilemma." Riggs traces "the development of competitive individualism versus intragroup social responsibility in the black community — a dilemma at the center of social stratification and black oppression today."[43] The moral dilemma is the following. Since the integration of blacks into white America in the 1960s, a black middle class has appeared within the

African American community. And this class division promotes individualism and a harmful competition among black folk. Riggs explores the late nineteenth- and early twentieth-century black women's club movement (in which Ida Wells-Barnett and Anna Julia Cooper were leaders) to determine some distinct socioreligious models for contemporary womanist ethical resolution of the moral dilemma.

To advance black liberation against white racism, male chauvinism, and capitalism, Riggs, working from the perspective of a person trained in ethics, offers a theoretical framework. Social stratification (i.e., class division) within the African American community, for her, comes from black oppression and needs to be addressed with intellectual analytical tools. "Parallel structures," the first plank in her theoretical outline, teach us how stratifications internal to the black community are parallel to the larger society. Second, "internal colonialism" helps us to understand black existence as similar to an oppressed colonial status. Colonizers control colonized communities by manipulating differences within those communities (similar to a divide-and-rule strategy). This is the reason nonblack people would work to increase conflicts among African Americans. Third, Riggs's theoretical framework includes the concept of a class-race-gender consciousness.

Riggs summarizes:

> The dilemma of competitive individualism versus intra-group social responsibility has its basis in both socio-economic realities and a race-class consciousness that has evolved throughout black history. The race-gender-class consciousness of black women offers an alternative perspective for analyzing this dilemma.[44]

Furthermore, Riggs believes that the justice of God and justice for blacks are God's commands and that their coming together create socioreligious responsibility. Therefore, on the one hand, justice (i.e., socioreligious responsibility replacing competitive individualism) affirms both black self-help and racial solidarity. On the other hand, it advocates self-determination within the larger American society.

Restated, justice as an ethic of socioreligious responsibility calls for "the specific aims of racial elevation, amelioration of gender and class oppression, and comprehensive reform of society for the good of all citizens."[45] With God's justice as the center of value in the African American community, womanist ethics provides a positive alternative "whereby accommodative and aggressive social activism, religious radicalism for societal change, and progress for individual Blacks and Blacks as a group could be maintained."[46]

The black women's club movement, Riggs also states, offers a three-part moral vision for the twenty-first century. The first element deals with the virtue of giving up one's privilege of difference, whether racial, gender, or class. The second component involves the value and obligation of inclusivity, which can take the form of all black women coming together across class lines. Ultimately, inclusivity connects work on behalf of black women to supporting the health of all black people, as well as struggling for justice for all. The third part of the moral vision is religious responsibility, the perspective and practice of linking racial uplift with God's justice. A womanist call for black liberation, consequently, will yield fruit when black women and the African American community act as moral agents toward their final aim. Riggs writes the following:

> Black liberation, therefore, refers to collective advancement of Blacks with the goal of transforming the economic and political structure of American society. The goal is ideologically nationalistic in that it emphasizes the need for black people to engender and sustain a communal identity. Black communal consciousness is critical to an ethic for black liberation. The contention here is that the social stratification of Blacks is a factor that undermines

black communal consciousness, and consequently, black liberation.[47]

Conclusion

Womanist theologians and ethicists have impacted and advanced black theology by their consistent and holistic call for recognition of all types of oppressions affecting the African American community and for the need for various approaches to resolve these theological and ethical problems. A unique contribution of black women is that their very lives make up an identity of gender, racial, and class strands within one body, mind, and spirit called the black woman. Womanists, moreover, have plowed persistently the diverse fields of black women's experience (and that of the overall black community) to cultivate lessons for today. Sources range from talking with friends to reading obscure scholarly texts. God appears and offers the grace of liberation and wholeness wherever God so chooses.

Finally, womanists have taken old religious language and symbols and given them new meaning. Womanists have called for a new witness in contrast to traditional theological categories and conclusions based on the dominant moral agency. Perhaps womanists will expand their holistic method, sources, and claims to produce extended treatments of a host of other topics, such as, the black body, ecology, and music.[48] Wholeness — a compassionate intellect and an intellectual passion — includes (1) the willingness to be led by the Spirit wherever it goes; (2) the interweaving of concern both for black women's realities and for the black community's predicament and possibilities; (3) the bridging of feminist and black liberation theologies; and (4) the connections to the poor class. All of these show us the practice and potential of womanist religious thought.

Chapter 5

Black Theology and Third World Liberation Theologies

In the late 1960s, when black theology of liberation was defining itself in the United States, similar liberation theologies began to arise throughout the Third World (i.e., in Africa, Asia, and Latin America). As black theology sought allies in its attempt to build a life that God had created for African Americans (i.e., to be full human beings) and to oppose the sin of white supremacy domestically, it met representatives from Africa, Asia, the Caribbean, and Latin America. These meetings brought renewed energy to black theology. In this process of dialoguing with liberation theologians around the world, basic agreements and commonalities, as well as initial tensions, came to the surface.

It is understandable that black theology of liberation would extend its interests and influence into the international arena. The idea of African Americans reaching out to African peoples all over the earth and extending acts of solidarity to the poor in the Third World was a central part of the 1960s and 1970s political and cultural demands of black folks' struggle for freedom and power. Both the prophetic Christianity of Martin Luther King Jr. (representing the civil rights movement) and the justice-based beliefs of Malcolm X (symbolizing the black power movement) advised black people and communities of faith to not limit their vision and organizing within the borders of the United States. The struggle of poor African Americans for full humanity and the movement for national liberation in the Third World were one.

For instance, a year before his assassination, King called for a global revolution of values. This was necessary, argued King, because the U.S. government, along with the monopoly capitalists who control the United States, carried out a simultaneous attack. Military acts against poor nations of color and the stealing of those nations' resources were similar to domestic capitalist police activities against the poor and people of color in the United States and the monopolizing of their wealth. To fight against racial discrimination and poverty at home, then, automatically led into a worldwide struggle. Linking the demonic nature of capitalism and its foreign investments, King stated:

> I have said that the problem, the crisis we face, is international in scope. In fact, it is inseparable from an international emergency which involves the poor, the dispossessed, and the exploited of the whole world.[1]

Even more directly, emphasizing his Pan-Africanist consciousness, King asserted:

> [I]njustice anywhere is a threat to justice everywhere, for we are tied together in a garment of mutuality. What happens in Johannesburg affects Birmingham.... We are descendants of the Africans. Our heritage is Africa. We should never seek to break the ties, nor should Africans.[2]

Similarly, Malcolm X called on black people to stretch forth their hands overseas, especially to Africa:

> You can't understand what is going on in Mississippi if you don't understand what is going on in the Congo. And you can't really be interested in what's going on in Mississippi if you're not also interested in what's going on in the Congo. They're both the same. The same interests are at stake.[3]

Malcolm connects, on the one hand, the black nationalist struggle of Africa's descendants in America against racial supremacy caused by Europe's descendants in America with, on the other hand, the national liberation struggle against European colonial control over the African continent. Africa was the root of black Americans' existence, and it was being strangled by a European capitalist and racist grip. Likewise, the fruit of Africa (i.e., black folk) suffered from that same stranglehold of white European offspring in the United States.

Black theology drew on these global and domestic interactions which were taking place in the civil rights and black power movements. Therefore, in a very natural way, black theology gravitated toward the victims of Portuguese colonialism and apartheid throughout the southern African region in the 1960s and 1970s. And it embraced the valiant effort of the Vietnamese people for liberation against U.S. imperialism. Consequently, when various liberation theologians from the underdeveloped world began to have meetings to form the Ecumenical Association of Third World Theologians (EATWOT) in 1976, African American theological and church leaders were ready for such an organization because black theology emerged from a context of struggle which was already standing in solidarity with the Third World.

Black Theology Meets African Theology

Prior to black theologians' official attendance at EATWOT conferences, the National Committee of Negro Churchmen (NCNC — founded in 1966, it was the first organization to develop black theology in the contemporary period) sent two observers to the 1969 assembly of the All Africa Conference of Churches (AACC) in Abidjan, Ivory Coast.[4] At this meeting African American delegates began to consciously link the movement for black power, the black church, and black theology in the United States with the developing liberation theology in Africa. As a result, the AACC decided to establish a "Round-Table Discussion on African Theology and Black Theology."

In 1971, Union Theological Seminary theologian James H. Cone, L. Maynard Catchings, chairperson of the Africa Commission of the NCBC (the National Committee of Negro Churchmen had now changed its name to the National Committee of Black Churchmen), and other black Americans met in Dar es Salaam, Tanzania, with African theologians and church leadership.[5] The Christian Council of Tanzania and the NCBC Africa Commission cosponsored this event under the theme "Black Identity and Solidarity and the Role of the Church as a Medium for Social Change," with a focus on economic development, education, and theology.

This conference marked the first time in contemporary black church history that African Americans and Africans had talked face-to-face without a white missionary go-between. At this meeting, the clear theological differences began to show. The twenty-eight black theologians accented the political "liberation" of the black poor, and the sixteen African scholars and church leaders underscored the importance of "Africanization," especially taking into account the importance of translating Christianity from European culture into African culture.

In January 1972, under the theme "African Theology and Church Life," at an African consultation at the Makerere University (Kampala), black religion scholar George Thomas (then an Interdenominational Theological Center professor in Atlanta) delivered a major presentation on the relation between black theology and African religion.

In June 1973 at Union Theological Seminary (New York City), another consultation was held between six African and twelve black American delegates. John S. Mbiti headed the African group, and C. Shelby Rooks (of the Society for the Study of Black Religion) led the black American contingent. As a result of this gathering, a larger meeting took place in December 1974 at the Ghana Institute for Management and Public Administration. On this occasion, the African delegates represented the theological commission of the AACC.[6] The theological debate between the political liberation of poor black Americans and the need to put the gospel message into African cultural forms (i.e., Africanization) continued.

The next meeting between African American theologians and their African counterparts took place in Accra, Ghana (December 1977). James H. Cone and Gayraud S. Wilmore, along with a small group of black Americans, attended this consultation sponsored by the Ecumenical Association of Third World Theologians (EATWOT) in connection with the Pan-African Conference of Third World Theologians. The debates between those emphasizing politics and culture and those emphasizing Africanization became even more focused. However, South African black theologians stood with the African American emphasis on political liberation.[7]

The first direct discussions between black theologians in the United States and South African black theologians occurred at Union Theological Seminary (New York City) in December 1986. James Cone's presentation framed three of the major theological issues at the conference: gender, race and class social analysis, and the authority of scripture in the development of a black theology of liberation. Regarding social analysis, Cornel West's speech argued for the necessity of dissecting the many levels of power in all societies: exploitation, subjugation, domination, and repression.

South African theologians added their insight as well. Simon S. Maimela called for the use of Marxist analysis in the process of doing theology. Itumeleng Mosala questioned whether or not there are two Gods in the Bible: a liberating one and a reactionary one.

Roxanne Jordan (South Africa) and Kelly Brown Douglas (United States) raised concerns about the black female identity of God. They developed theologies from black women's unique experiences in their respective countries. Both Jordan and Brown showed how God and Christ revealed themselves in black women's political and cultural experiences. Together, they painted an integral womanist–black feminist theological process. Attacking the evils of exploitation based on gender, race, and class, black women across the Atlantic were creating a vibrant theology by combining political and cultural sources.[8]

In August 1993, EATWOT sponsored a conference on the globalization of black theology. Held in South Africa, the conference focused on the dialogue between black theology in the United States and in South Africa. Issues of concern included culture, politics, women, the Bible and theology, and theology and social analysis. The agenda contained presentations from U.S. and South African theologians on the same topic as a way of organizing the dialogue between the black voices. This gathering generated several important theological developments.

First, it used a more comprehensive social analysis in black theology internationally because politics, economics, class, race, gender, sexual orientation, African indigenous religions, and African culture were all discussed and not pitted against each other. Second, black women from both sides of the Atlantic made their presence known by the presentations they gave, by the recurrence of (American) womanist and (South African black) feminist theological themes throughout the conference, and by the numbers of black women in both delegations.

Third, though the focus was on the United States and South Africa, black theologians attended also from Australia, Canada, the Caribbean, England, India, Latin America, the Netherlands, New Zealand, the Pacific Islands, and other countries in Africa. In the history of American black theology's relation to the continent of Africa, the close ties between South Africa and black Americans around the issues of political liberation and the beauty of God's gift of blackness have encouraged a consistent and deep dialogue. This has helped to clarify the commonalities and differences between black theology in the United States and African theology.[9]

The commonalities and differences between black theology in the United States and African theology vary.[10] First, both have much in their common ancestry. African Americans are not simply Americans — they are Americans with a difference. It is precisely this difference, this African difference, that continually reminds black people of their origin in their motherland, which is Africa. If there was sufficient documentation, many blacks in the United States would be able to directly trace their family background to Africa, especially the West Coast. In that sense, black Americans still have distant family and blood ties to the Continent.

In addition, black theology and African theology share a common history of struggle against white supremacy and its relation to the Christian gospel. Enslaved blacks in North America and Africans in their own homeland were introduced to the Bible by European missionaries. This suggests a permanent negative commonality. Both sides of the Atlantic encountered the white supremacist attitudes and practices of whites from Europe and their descendants in North America. Whites introduced the Bible to blacks and Africans if they accepted the status of slavery, a subhuman position, or imitated white people.

Consequently, African Americans and Africans have from the very first day of contact with Europeans and whites experienced racial oppression and arrogance. To become Christian, the test was to give up one's black and African identities along with one's natural resources. In return, the black person received white culture and was fitted into the white imperialist and slave economy as an exploited worker. An African common wisdom saying states that when European Christian missionaries came to the Continent, they asked the Africans to pray. When all were through and opened up their eyes, white Christians had taken black people's land and other natural resources in addition to opposing African indigenous culture. In return, Africans were left with the Bible and the clothing, culture, and capitalist individualistic lifestyles of Europe.

A similar process took place with enslaved African Americans. They received the Bible and white culture and were left without their full African culture. The introduction of Christianity meant white supremacy and arrogance and an attempt to take away wealth, resources, and black ways of being in the world. Both faced the questions: Could one be black and Christian? Could one be an African Christian? In other words, did Africans and African Americans have to imitate Europeans and whites to become Christians?

Black North American theology and African theology both reject the oppressive interpretations of God from Europe and the United States, especially forms of liberal and conservative faith systems. Black theologians ask why and how it is possible for white Americans to do theology without taking seriously the history and ongoing reality of African American suffering. African theologians reject oppressive theologies that tend to define African indigenous religions and cultures as subhuman, superstitious, or barbaric.

While victimized by a racist Christianity and theology, black and African theologies share a revolutionary reinterpretation of this distorted view of the gospel. They did not allow victimization to stop their God-given right to be their own proactive agents and actors in this world. Through their own reinterpretations, enslaved African Americans created the foundation for a black theology of liberation in North America. They carried this out in the Invisible Institution, the secret religious meetings of blacks during slavery. Africans took European and American missionary perspectives on the Bible and placed them within the context of African indigenous cultures, which existed prior to the arrival of European colonialism.

A final commonality is the rise of black and African women's voices onto the theological scene. In the United States, we find this reality in the development of womanist theology. On the Continent, this new reality was demonstrated by the election in 1996 of Mercy Amba Oduyoye (from Ghana) as president of EATWOT. She was the first woman elected to the office.

Commonalities have not blocked the surfacing of differences. The African American experience is that of a minority population, stripped of its original land in Africa, removed from its African indigenous language, and forced to forget the memory of its ancestors in Africa. In contrast, the African experience is of a majority population whose memory of their ancestors remains in the grave sites and stories handed down to each generation through bloodlines and family storytellers. Africans are on the land which has been in their possession for centuries. Therefore, they do not suffer from historical amnesia as much as black Americans. They can trace their ancestry back for centuries. They, in addition, have a language completely different from Americans and Europeans. And perhaps most importantly, they have access to indigenous cultures and religions.

Black theology in the United States asks the question: What does God have to do with my blackness as a minority in a system of white supremacy? African theology poses the question: As a majority population with a vast indigenous culture, language, and religion, how can I accept Christianity through my own indigenous culture?

However, the united front (around culture) in African theology is not as closed as we would think. Black theology in South Africa, like its counterpart in the United States, emphasizes political liberation and holds that the heart of the gospel message is liberation of the poor. Further, black theology from the United States (in the form of James H. Cone's *Black Theology and Black Power*)[11] was a source for the emergence of South African black theology. Because white supremacy was structurally part of the American power-structure and because South African society was also built on institutionalized white-skin privileges, black South Africans could accept American black theology more easily.

At the same time, the dominance of black theology should not obscure other expressions of theology in South Africa. For instance, there has been a strong Africanization or indigenization movement led by such scholars as Gabriel M. Setiloane of Botswana and South Africa. His *African Theology: An Introduction* puts him in line with churches and theologians outside South Africa who are less concerned with politics, economics, and class (i.e., key elements in black theology) and more concerned with language, ancestors, and indigenous rituals (i.e., key elements in African theology).[12]

Just as South African black scholars have different approaches to theology, so too do scholars in the rest of the Continent. In contrast to the general agreement among scholars who do African theology by following the Africanization process (i.e., the search to make the gospel relevant to African indigenous culture and religions), we find echoes of a stress on political liberation in certain French-speaking African countries to the north of South Africa.[13]

Still, in general, we can say that during the first period of contact, black theology in the United States emphasized the political dimensions of the gospel of Jesus Christ. This faith approach looked at systems of oppression and liberation in terms of economic and political power. American black theologians saw blackness (e.g., the experiences of poor and working-class black folk) as the main place where God revealed God's self to oppressed humanity. Consequently, God worked through blackness to help in the liberation process. Moreover, black theologians suspected that African theology's stress on culture meant that African scholars and church leaders were too conservative and probably supporters of capitalism. When black theology in the United States met Latin American theology, black Americans stressed race and culture and Latin Americans cited class and politics.

Black Theology Meets Latin American Theology

Black theology of liberation in the United States and Latin American theology of liberation began independent of each other.[14] While Latin American scholars (especially Gustavo Gutiérrez in his 1971 original edition of *A Theology of Liberation*)[15] were connecting liberation to the Christian faith of the poor in their region of the Americas, black theologians (especially James H. Cone in his 1969 *Black Theology and Black Power* and then his 1970 *A Black Theology of Liberation*)[16] were experiencing and defining liberation as the essence of Jesus' gospel in North America. Both groups of scholars, thus, were constructing liberation theologies without knowledge of the other.

However, Latin American scholars emphasized class struggle while blacks asserted the liberation of the black poor around race. For Latin American theologians, the question was: What does the gospel of liberation have to say about class exploitation? For black theologians, the question was: What does the gospel of liberation have to do with racial oppression of the African American poor?

The year 1973 proved crucial to the start of dialogue between black and Latin American theologies. At that time, Cone's *A Black Theology of Liberation* became available in a Spanish edition.[17] In the same year, Orbis Books published Gutiérrez's text in English. And May 1973 saw the first important dialogue between black theology of liberation and Latin American liberation theology. This meeting took place at a conference sponsored by the World Council of Churches (WCC) in Geneva, Switzerland. Wanting to learn more about black and Latin American theologies, the WCC invited two spokespersons from each discipline. Eventually the discussions and debates with the Europeans and white Americans present led the black and Latin American participants to conclude that they should be dialoguing alone, without whites in attendance.[18]

The significance of Geneva is that both groups of liberation theologians warmly agreed that their commonalities called for future talks between them. Also, mutual conversation in a face-to-face format without Europeans was held to be an important goal. Latin Americans even confessed their being overly influenced by Western training, culture, and theology. Consequently, the black religious experience had been invisible in their thinking, at worst, or, at best, it had been seen through the eyes of white Westerners. Finally, Latin American theologians referred to blacks as part of the Third World, which implied a solidarity between the poor in Africa, Asia, and Latin America, on the one hand, and oppressed blacks in a First World monopoly capitalist country, on the other.

However, this feeling of mutual solidarity began to weaken. In August 1975, Sergio Torres, a Latin American theologian, organized a conference in Detroit in order to introduce Latin American theology to white North Americans. Black theological and church leaders were left out of the planning of this meeting. This seemed to contradict the feeling, mood, and agreement of the 1973 Geneva meeting, where Latin theologians wanted to enter into dialogue with blacks because too much conversation had already taken place with Europeans and white North Americans. Now, Latin Americans not only were starting conversations with white North Americans but were establishing institutional relations. The Detroit meeting formed Theology in the Americas (TIA), which, because of the struggle of the few blacks and other people of color present, became the first multiracial liberation theology group in the United States in the contemporary period.[19]

At this meeting, African Americans claimed that racial discrimination and the struggle for racial freedom were key issues in the historical and current analysis of the United States. In contrast, the Latin Americans consistently focused on the importance of the capitalist mode of production and distribution and on class as the primary issues in North American social relations. Because blacks at the conference did not use Marxism as a tool of social analysis and did not advocate socialism as the goal of the black theology and black church struggle, Latin Americans wanted to know if black theology was simply a supporter of bourgeois monopoly capitalism. This larger system created cultural, political, economic, and racial discrimination. Oppression based on race, therefore, was fruit from the tree of capitalist exploitation. To stop it from bearing poisonous fruit, the Latin Americans said, the tree had to be cut down.

In opposition to this theological analysis, the very few black participants (who had been allowed to attend by the Latin Americans organizers) argued against any description of North American society which excluded, downplayed, or ignored the central role of race in white folks' discrimination against African Americans.

James H. Cone described the new direction which Latin American theology took in its relation to black theology of liberation when he cited at least two reasons for his and other African American participants' reluctance to accept the particular class analysis offered at the conference. First, the history of the white Christian left was one of extreme racism and arrogance in the United States. At the conference, nearly two hundred white Christians were defining the nature of liberation theology and oppression and resistance in the United States. Why were white North Americans so radical about class, as it emerged in the Latin American context, while these same whites enjoyed their white-skin privileges and white power over African Americans in their own country? To Cone and other people of color, it seemed that white Christians were very willing to pursue justice against the exploitation and oppression all over the rest of the world, but were not interested in fighting the exploitation and oppression which white Christians themselves had created in their own country, the United States.

Second, Latin American delegates at the Detroit meeting were white people (in contrast to the millions of blacks and Indians in South and Central America) and showed a white supremacist and arrogant attitude that was similar to that of the white North American Christians at the meeting. The Latin Americans had come to North America, and instead of talking with the victims of white supremacy and the leaders of resistance movements in the United States (e.g., blacks, the African American church, and other people of color), they sought conversations with those who perpetuated the sin of racism. White Latin Americans, it seemed, did not believe that black folk could think theologically and therefore did not have much to contribute to doing liberation theology throughout the Americas.

Furthermore, what was it that allowed Latin Americans to work with the poor in their own context but kept them from seeing U.S. blacks as being among the poorest of the poor? It seemed by not being consistent in their own theology (that is to say, Jesus Christ liberates the poor in Latin America but not the *black* poor in the United States), Latin Americans were gravitating to the white Christian left because both had in common white skin, white culture, and white theology.

Latin Americans left the meeting believing blacks were North American capitalists and cultural nationalists who failed to see the international implications of class struggle. African Americans felt that Latin Americans were white supremacists. Fortunately, due to their common faith in the gospel of liberation, both sides continued to carry out dialogue in diverse ways before their next gathering in Mexico City in 1977.

James H. Cone cites the positive role played by Sergio Torres (from Chile), who eventually helped in the reorganization of TIA, which led to more empowerment of the people of color.[20] Similarly, Gustavo Gutiérrez (from Peru, and often referred to as the father of Latin American liberation theology) expressed deep sensitivity to the status of black folk in the United States and the role of the African American church and black theology in the movement for African Americans' full humanity. As a visiting professor at Union Theological Seminary in 1976, he engaged in long and lively conversations with James H. Cone (and other black Christians) over the importance of culture and history for African American life today.

In a similar fashion, representing black theology of liberation in the United States, James H. Cone accepted an invitation to Mexico City to be a presenter at the Encounter of Theologians in October 1977. His lecture and the following discussions indicated a willingness on the part of African Americans to take seriously class analysis, imperialism, and the relationship between race and globalization as crucial ingredients in the doing of black theology in North America.[21] At the same time, the response of the audience showed the opening by Latin Americans to hear and embrace the particular reality of African Americans. The harsh accusations against North American blacks as bourgeois and narrow nationalists were replaced with their acceptance as oppressed allies.

The Latin American critique remains important because it asks crucial questions about the definition of the concept "Third World." Does it refer to geography (e.g., Africa, Asia, the Caribbean, Latin America, and the Pacific Islands, thus excluding African Americans)? Or does it mean a situation of exploitation and dependence (a definition that would necessitate accepting the full participation and status of African Americans on the global scene and extending acts of solidarity)?

Likewise, the race and class debate has deepened the sensitivity of the theologians and has necessitated a more comprehensive understanding of how Jesus Christ's gospel impacts the freedom of all in North America and Latin America. In North America, black folk's subjection to white supremacy is directly linked to an institution of monopoly capitalism — that is, bourgeois democracy for the small group of white families who own and control the means of production and most of the wealth in the United States. In Latin America, an effective gospel of full humanity results from using class analysis as well as the culture and history of black Latin Americans and indigenous populations.

Black Theology Meets Asian Theology

Black theologians have had less contact with Asian theologians than with Latin American theologians. Part of this lack of dialogue comes from ignorance. In the United States, most black people either have no contact with Asians or assume that Asian merchants in the black community are immigrants who are not interested in the history and culture of African Americans. Moreover, lack of global theological conversation results from the geographical distance between the two regions. African Americans have a strong tradition of traveling to Africa, the Caribbean, and Latin America, but not to Asia. Finally, because only 2 percent of the Asian population is Christian, black people do not have a tradition of turning to Christians in Asia for conversations.

James H. Cone was the earliest and has been the most consistent dialogue partner in the discussions between U.S. black theology of liberation and Asian theologies. Cone accepted an invitation from the Korean Christian Church in Japan to be a workshop leader at a conference titled "The Church Struggling for the Liberation of the People" in May 1975. In Japan, Cone saw an Asian minority population (the Korean Japanese) suffering discrimination from the majority population (the Japanese), and he immediately understood the commonalities between Korean-Japanese theology and American black theology. In his reflection on the similarities, he writes:

> In Japan, it was not difficult to perceive the similarities between the Korean experience in that country and the black

experience in the United States. As blacks were stolen from Africa by Europeans and enslaved in the Americas, Koreans were taken against their will from their homeland and brought to Japan in order to serve Japanese people. Like blacks who expressed their struggle for justice by creating songs of liberation derived from the biblical account of the Exodus, Korean Christians in Japan expressed their determination to be free in a similar fashion. As blacks experience discrimination in employment and in every other aspect of American society, Koreans have an analogous experience in Japan.[22]

Blacks in North America experienced racism and arrogance from whites, and Koreans in Japan suffered a similar racism and arrogance from Japanese. Whites and Japanese were more open to theologies coming from Europe and less interested in the prophetic nature of the gospel of Jesus Christ.

In contrast, blacks and Koreans embraced Jesus' message of liberation and power for the least in society. We should note that four years later (May 1979), Cone returned to Japan at the invitation of Japanese activists focused on children's issues. Unlike the predominantly middle-class Japanese he met in 1975, those who invited him in 1979 included a Japanese citizen's group fighting for the survival and improved quality of life of oppressed children. Consequently, Cone could identity black theology with certain segments of Japanese society focused on compassion for, the oppression of, and the struggle for the liberation of the least in Japanese society.

After the 1975 conference in Japan, Cone flew to Seoul, Korea, where a state of emergency had been called by the dictator, Park Chung Hee. Because of the presence of the Korean CIA, he decided to speak on the African American situation as reflected in the Negro spirituals, thereby taking attention away from the direct issues facing Korean Christians and activists in the audience. For the same reason, no questions and discussions were allowed after his lecture. However, during private conversations with many Korean Christians and after observing the similarities between the political dictatorship of the Park regime and the white supremacist system in the United States, Cone saw a deep connection between Korean liberation theology and U.S. black theology.

First, by using songs from the African American civil rights movement, Korean Christians drew on the religion and culture of black folk in order to inform their own prophetic faith. Second, the life-and-death situation in which Korean Christians and others lived deepened Cone's appreciation that the gospel of Jesus Christ is not neutral on earth. We have to take a stand for those facing political oppression or any other type of supremacy. After faith leads one to stand with the oppressed, theology becomes the second step — the step of reflecting on one's prior political commitment with the poor and society's vulnerable.

In January 1979, Cone attended the Asian Theological Conference in Sri Lanka, which brought together seventy-five delegates representing eleven Asian countries (including the Fiji Islands). This group included Protestants, Roman Catholics, Buddhists, and Muslims. Africa, the United States, and Latin America sent two fraternal delegates each, and the Caribbean had one representative. Perhaps this meeting exhibited the richest learning process for black theology of liberation.[23]

This broader exposure of black theology to the complicated realities of Asia helped to deepen an appreciation for allowing theology to arise from the particularity of each situation. By starting the conference with a three-day live-in with poor people in Sri Lanka and by limiting the number of non-Asian delegates (particularly from Latin America), Asian theologians made a clear statement against importing European and North American theologies into this region of the world.

Moreover, the complexity of Asia became clear in the persistence of its ancient and great religions — such as Taoism, Confucianism, Shamanism, Buddhism, Hinduism, Jainism, Islam, and Shintoism. The Asian reality is dominated by its own unique religions and cultures, distinct from those of the West. Therefore, to talk about God's revelation only through Jesus Christ became absurd in Asia, the largest population in the world. It suggested that Asia was a heathen territory with pagan religions and did not enjoy the presence of God's liberation and salvation for the poor.

On the contrary, the minority status of Christianity pointed out how God's presence to oppressed humanity knew no boundaries. The overwhelming number of ancient religions and cultures testified to divine presence. And if Christianity were to spread in the region, it had to take seriously the beliefs, traditions, spirituality, and rituals of these religions and cultures.

In addition, and most important, the Asian region contained all the theological issues which segments of EATWOT had only grasped partially. Asia was confronted with the class and political concerns of Latin America, the indigenous cultures and religions asserted by Africa, and the racial line of demarcation that defined both North America and South Africa. Indeed, Asian liberation theologians argued for a many-sided analysis of God's presence in the world, which meant that divine liberation is revealed in all religions, cultures, societies, and politics that work to achieve the full humanity of the oppressed.

Examples of the various dimensions of the Asian reality were these: the local states of political repression, exploitation of workers by foreign multinational corporations (mainly U.S.), the overwhelming presence of layers upon layers of poverty, the clear and daily rituals of Asia's own religions (and the near absence of Christianity in Asia, except in the Philippines), and the unique cultures and way of life in contrast to the West. Theologians and laypeople in Asia could not separate any of these aspects of their lives and say which one was primary and which could be left out. In Asia, theologically speaking, the world was one.

Black theology had met a diverse group of partners in conversation and solidarity throughout the Third World. In the initial meeting with African theology, black theology critiqued it for being too bourgeois in its emphasis on culture and too conservative for not condemning unjust economic institutions. In the first contact with Latin American theology, black theology raised forcefully the importance of culture and indigenous religions over against dogmatic Marxism and the exclusive use of class analysis applied by the Latin American scholars. In its beginning connections with Asian theology, black theology discovered the importance of God's revelation for the full humanity of the poor expressed in a comprehensive fabric of politics, culture, social relations, and religions.

Black Theology and EATWOT

African American Christians have been in attendance at all major meetings of the Ecumenical Association of Third World Theologians (EATWOT), the only organization of liberation theologians from Africa, Asia, the Caribbean, Latin America, the Pacific Islands, and North America.

The origin of the concept for an international dialogue among theologians in Africa, Asia, and Latin America came from Abbe Oscar K. Bimwenyi, a Roman Catholic student from Zaire studying theology in Louvain, Belgium, in 1974.[24] As a result of his vision and the preparatory committees composed of representatives from Africa, Asia, and Latin America, the organizing conference which gave rise to the Ecumenical Dialogue of Third World Theologians (later Dialogue changed to Association) took place in Dar es Salaam, Tanzania, in August 1976. Since that time, EATWOT has held different continental and intercontinental dialogues engaging the specific focus of Africa, Asia, and Latin America. And it has taken up the theological significance of race, indigenous peoples, and Third World women.[25]

Differences remain in EATWOT — Africans accent theology, culture, and indigenous religions; Latin Americans argue for a class analysis informed by Marxist insights; and Asians assert a religio-cultural and sociopolitical approach to faith and the poor. Women continue to press that they are made in the image of God. And indigenous peoples, especially those in Latin America, North America, Australia, and New Zealand, continue to put forth their theological voices. Still, general agreement exists among all participants, including black theologians.[26]

First, all liberation theologians agree that God reveals God's self among the poor, in their status of oppression, in their worship of God, and in their movement for liberation and full humanity. Second, if the vocation of the theologian is to point out the presence of divine revelation and this revelation of God's purpose is found with the poor, then the theologian and the Christian church must side with the indigenous religions, cultures, and political plight of the poor. In other words, theologians and churches need to make a commitment to the least in society and against those systems and structures of society maintaining the subordination of the majority of people.

Third, theology is reflection on this commitment to and practice and worship with the least in society; theology is a second step. This second step does not entail the solitary scholar or church leader attempting to correlate the divine biblical message of liberation with the signs of the times for the poor today. On the contrary, just as the first step of commitment and practice is communal, so too is the moment of reflection. With others engaged in the process for full humanity, the theologian and church leader opens herself and himself up to criticism and self-criticism from those who both affirm and disagree.

Moreover, reflection means determining where and how God's liberation reveals itself. To assist us in understanding this revelation in society, we need various ways of analyzing the world. That is why liberation theologians in EATWOT call for investigating who has power based on race, gender, class, and control of ecology (i.e., the earth's natural resources). God presents God's self in the concrete social relationships of racial oppression, sexual discrimination, and economic exploitation. Social analysis and theology go together.

Fourth, from the position of the poor in history, liberation theology, working with the poor, rereads Hebrew and Christian Scriptures and discovers a thread of liberation as the core message of the Bible. The Hebrew Scriptures (e.g., the book of Exodus and the various Hebrew prophets) celebrate Yahweh siding with a group of slaves, delivering them from evil institutions, and helping them into a new land. The Christian Scriptures (e.g., Luke 4:18ff.; Matt. 25:31ff.) point to God's revelation in Jesus Christ, who came to set free the poor and oppressed throughout the world and usher in God's new Common Wealth for all humanity. To be faithful to God's word in the Bible is to work with the Holy Spirit empowering the poor in history on earth now.

Fifth, since EATWOT's first gathering in Dar es Salaam in 1976, its meetings have always participated in and given emphasis to the sacredness of worship of God: prayer, spirituality, and biblical study. Theology concerns worship and spiritual activities because the faith of the poor in Jesus Christ is fundamentally one of giving thanks for the grace of liberation offered by God to the least in society against the arrogance of principalities and powers on earth. The Bible has proven to be key in the ongoing reinvigoration of EATWOT. It is this written testimony which enables hope in a resurrected new humanity in the future. And this hope helps the poor to struggle now on earth for God's new Common Wealth promised in the Hebrew and Christian Scriptures.

Spirituality shows itself differently throughout the Third World. EATWOT theologians, for instance, here pointed out that spirituality is God's spirit of liberation moving among the poor in action and contemplation, in prayer and meditation, in word and silence, in song and dance, in nature and history, in the church and outside the church, in ancient religions and in Christianity, and in the ancestors and the unborn.

Sixth, all theologies are contextual. They emerge out of the particular context of a certain region of the world, country, nation, people, or local community. Therefore, liberation theologians reject the types of universal claims put forward by European scholars and white North Americans. These academics and church leaders fail to recognize that all talk about God is already filtered through specific cultures and class interests. EATWOT does not accept any prefabricated or top-down theologies from the United States or Europe. In this sense, Third World theologians use an inductive method for discerning God's revelations for full humanity. We do not start with an abstract and general definition of revelation. On the contrary, EATWOT members seek divine revelation as it is incarnated in the culture, religion, politics, and economics of the poor.

Black theology and other forms of liberation theologies offer critiques of white North American and European theology in order to clear the path for a more authentic practice and reflection in the interests of the world's majority (e.g., people of color and the poor in the Third World). A universal liberation theology, if such a thing is hoped for, would thus have to be based in the daily lives of the world's majority who are poor and of color.

In addition, liberation theologians want to make clear that humans, not God, do theology. Though this statement might seem like common sense, it is, in fact, a radical critique of traditional European and white North American theology. It is an eye-opener and a breath of fresh air for the poor and others who are marginalized in society. For too long, those at the bottom have been told that they could not think and that their experiences with God are not important or decisive. They have been told that their histories are not valid.

But now liberation theology asserts that the faith of the poor in the experience of God's liberation must move to the center stage of history. The poor, like European and white North American theologians, are human, and therefore they can also think and do theology. The affirmation of poor humanity's theological experience with God is subversive precisely because this allows the poor to no longer be dependent on the authority of traditional dominant theology. Once the poor and oppressed sections of society become independent theologically, assured of their own experience and their own story, and continue to pursue God's demand for liberation, they have the potential to change the status quo.

Finally, Jesus Christ offers love, liberation, and salvation for all of humanity who accept the gospel and side with the poor. Jesus Christ's work of love, liberation, and salvation shows itself among particular poor communities. And in those communities or struggles for full humanity we see Christ's universal love, liberation, and salvation. Therefore, the universal and the particular, the spiritual and the physical, and God's salvation history and human history all come together in specific movements of the oppressed. Black theology of liberation and Third World liberation theologies agree that all of humanity is freed when the majority of the world, who are poor and marginalized, are freed.

Chapter 6

Conclusion

This introduction to black theology of liberation has developed different aspects of the question: What does it mean to be black and Christian? Is there a unique relationship between being black in North America and, at the same time, believing in, worshiping, and following the way of the God of freedom, through the example of Jesus Christ the liberator and the ongoing empowerment of the Holy Spirit? All African American Christians need to struggle with these questions. However, there is a particular role for black theology. A black theology of liberation is that part of the church which attempts to assess the extent to which given beliefs and practices reflect what God wants Christians to believe and do. Black theology is that part of the church which is consciously and intentionally raising questions of accountability. In conversation and practice with the African American church, it helps the church understand the presence of the divine Spirit among the least in the African American community.

In response to the issue of being black and Christian, black theology has discovered that the vocation for the African American community, in particular the black church, is to work, in light of Jesus Christ, for the full spiritual and material humanization and liberation of the black oppressed and against racism. Likewise, this vocation calls on the black church to work for the full liberation of all people from that which denies their relationship with God. God wants the black poor and marginalized to be delivered from internal and external obstacles that would keep them from being completely what God has created them to be — full human beings able to reach their full God-given potential.

The role of black theology, therefore, is to work with the poor and marginalized in the African American church and community in order to remind us of this specific calling and instruction from God. Black theology helps the African American oppressed claim their blackness and their freedom as children of God. With that faith, they can move through both personal and collective demons on the spiritual and material levels. Theologically speaking, the God of the Hebrew Scriptures who worked with slaves to bring about the exodus is the same God who in the Christian Scriptures healed the brokenhearted, removed their pains, and lifted up the downtrodden from spiritual constraints and material systems of exploitation.

That same God lives today among the black poor and marginalized and lifts up their spirits in order for them to struggle against systemic principalities and powers on earth. If the God of the Bible wills to be with the least in society and also wills this purpose for all of humanity, then black theology works with the African American church to be where God is — among the bottom sections of the African American community. Thus the specific insight of a black theology of liberation is that the revelation of God's good news of a free full humanity presents itself in the texture and rhythm of oppressed black people's struggle for a liberated humanity. To be black and Christian, in this sense, is to open oneself and to turn one's full self to God's will.

In chapter 1, we examined this process of openness and turning as it is manifested in four building blocks that go into the construction of black theology of liberation. We started with the historical interaction between a God of freedom and the enslaved African and black experience in North America (1619–1865). And we discovered that enslaved black workers created a new faith and witness from the memory of their

African indigenous religions, folk wisdom from the everyday life experience of oppression and the fight for freedom, and a reinterpretation of the Christianity introduced to them by their white Christian slave masters. This new black religion of faith and practice planted the seeds for a radical way of thinking about what God had called African American workers to believe in and do. The critical reflection on the faith of the good news led to an outline of a black theology (e.g., theology continually reminds an oppressed community about God's instructions for their spiritual and material liberation).

In addition to slave religion, a new reading of the Bible — the next aspect in the development of black theology — has been operating since the period of slavery until today. The spiritually empowered oppressed black community brings its own life experiences to a reading of the Bible. Thus authority of interpretation hinges on the location of the readers as they experience God in their own place on this earth. The subversive nature of this type of rereading lies precisely in dismissing the automatic claims of biblical interpretation on the part of those who try to hold down the oppressed.

Moreover, if the oppressed claim their own authority to interpret the Bible, they are better able to assert their authority in other areas of society. The God of the Hebrew and Christian Scriptures serves as the highest court of judgment which can empower the oppressed to dismiss the sinful and demonic claims of the oppressor as a lesser authority. In other words, when the least in society are freed psychologically and theologically to take a risk and proclaim their own power of reinterpreting the Bible, this process of defiance and liberation can help them to really see God — not human beings who hold power on earth or the oppressed's own internal spiritual demons causing pain within their own souls — as their ultimate judge.

The third and most intentional building block of a black theology of liberation was the work of the civil rights and black power movements in the 1950s, 1960s, and 1970s. The civil rights movement, led by the black church and such pioneers as Rosa Parks, Martin Luther King Jr., and Fannie Lou Hamer, redefined further the nature of the Bible and the Christian church. Black janitors, maids, nannies, and industrial and rural workers provided the backbone for the civil rights struggle. Their personal faith in a biblical God who would never leave them alone gave the sustaining power to the movement. As they sang freedom songs in churches throughout the South and as they marched through the backwoods of the rural South, they believed that the liberator God of the Hebrew and Christian Scriptures was with them in their struggle.

Similarly, along with the formal leadership figures of the civil rights movement, these same working-class blacks extended the notion of the African American church from singing, praying, and worshiping in a building to the act of marching in the streets. Thus the Bible took on a deeper meaning, and the church was transformed from just a Sunday eleven A.M. gathering to a daily way of life to attain the full human and divine rights of African Americans.

The black power movement challenged the idea of what it meant to be black in America. Previously, an African American person was expected to imitate and worship all things from the white community. But new voices raised the importance of the beauty of blackness — of African Americans' hair texture, skin color, facial features, music, poetry, language, values, and connections to Africa. One of the prominent contributions of black power advocates was the assertion that it was good to be black — a revolutionary notion for most of America. African Americans did not have to imitate white Americans in order to be considered civilized or even human beings. It was Malcolm X, more than any other figure, who unraveled African Americans' psychological chains of self-hate and shame. Malcolm preached the following: the worst thing the white community had done to the black community was to teach it to hate its own self. Malcolm encouraged his followers to love their own black and African selves, which were created by a black God. Lastly, the black power advocates stated that African American people needed and deserved power like any other ethnic group in America.

On July 31, 1966, a group of African American clergy published their Christian interpretation of black power. Basically they combined the civil rights notion of a redefined Bible and church with the black power conception of the need for black affirmation and power. Three years later, the first theological statement which positioned liberation at the heart of the gospel message was published — James H. Cone's *Black Theology and Black Power*. Black theology, in particular, and African American religion, in general, had shifted to a new level.

The final building block we examined in chapter 1 was method. Method, as a construction of a black theology of liberation, enables the African American church to carry out what God has called the church to believe in, preach, and do in this world. In this sense, method is a dynamic process which helps the oppressed to respond to God's calling to be fully free and liberated human beings.

Method entails identifying the sources where God is already present. We discovered several sources: the Bible, black church tradition, the legacy of struggle for liberation outside and inside the church, African American women, culture, and radical politics. Method also asks about the norm which allows us to determine where in the sources God is revealing God's will of liberation. Furthermore, the norm judges which sources we should start with. Not everything in the black experience, community, church, and family is liberating. Coupled with sources and norm, the actual rhythm of doing theology rounds out its method. The first aspect of this rhythm is working in solidarity with the least in society because that is where the divine can already be found. Next is theological reflection about one's prior practice. And third is a return to a liberating practice of faith now deepened by critical theological reflection. And so the rhythm of the method continues today and in the future.

Then chapter 2 examined the first contemporary theologians who attempted to look more deeply at the actual content of black theology. This first generation of African American theologians, working in the 1960s to the beginning of the 1980s, divided into a political wing and a cultural wing.

The political wing answered the question of how being black and Christian relates to issues of power and the right of self-determination. These theologians chose to explore the traditional areas of systematic theology and the Christian church. They wanted to know how faith revealed itself in politics; they opposed racism in the predominantly white political system, theological academy, and church gatherings. We saw how James H. Cone argued for liberation as the heart of the Christian message and J. Deotis Roberts claimed liberation and reconciliation together as the core thread of the good news.

In contrast, the cultural wing chose to explore how faith is manifested in African American culture. They condemned white supremacist cultural structures of religion and theology. They critiqued the political wing for simply accepting and adopting the theological structures of white Christians and, thereby, simply adding black content to these oppressive structures. Instead, the cultural theologians advocated a focus on the African side of the African American experience. Gayraud S. Wilmore supported the notion of a black religion that was broader than black theology and that included acts of faith that mainstream Christians might call non-Christian or heretical. His point was that wherever God revealed belief in and acts of liberation, there one found black religion, inside and outside the church, and inside and outside Christianity. Charles H. Long suggested a need to look at black religious language. Rather than focus on black theology, which he felt supported the racism of white theology because it adopted and thereby was trapped by that theology's language structures, he advanced the idea of looking at the unique language and symbols found throughout the African American community, especially as these languages and symbols related to the holy (i.e., the ultimate concern).

The strength of the cultural wing was its concern for the unique parts of what it meant to be black and Christian. So it focused specifically on the African part of the black identity. Wherever a faith and practice of liberation existed, there one discovered the revelation of God. Consequently, in African American history and today, the cultural theologians saw divine examples both inside and outside the church. Moreover, they correctly underscored one unique reality of black Americans; that is, they are an African people and have a special connection to the African continent.

In contrast, the contribution of the political wing was its recognition of systemic power and how it impacted the definition of being black and Christian in the church and in the field of systematic theology. Perhaps the greatest hope for transformation of the status of African Americans today comes from the black church. Despite its flaws, it remains a beacon of hope for millions of black Americans. Because systematic theology focuses on raising critical questions to the black church about the nature of its divine calling, the political theologians were correct in emphasizing and redefining systematic theology as a discipline. In fact, the political and cultural wings agreed on the plumb line of liberation of the poor and the least in society. Their differences showed complementary ways of how to lay this plumb line.

Chapter 3 explored how the first generation has produced a second generation of black theologians and religious scholars. The growth of the second generation was indicated by the publication of two essays in 1979. First, Jacquelyn Grant, in her "Black Theology and the Black Woman," asked about the absence of African American women in the writings and concerns of the first-generation black theologians. In her assessment, the first generation of black men had made women invisible. Either the political and cultural wings thought women were invisible, or they thought their male voices spoke for women. Moreover, stated Grant, not only were black women missing in black theology, but black theology itself was inconsistent because it called for liberation for the poor but continued to oppress African American women. In addition, black theology was an elitist Christian movement because it kept the majority of the members of the African American church and community from speaking their voice. Black women comprised 70 to 80 percent of most churches and over half the entire African American community.

The second essay, Cornel West's "Black Theology and Marxist Thought," challenged the first generation about the exact nature of its definition of the poor. For West, a philosopher of religion, the objective method and analysis of Marxism showed that class, specifically the African American working class, had to be at the forefront of black theology's efforts. If the political and cultural wings of the first generation did not define the poor specifically as working people, then black theology would simply be another form of a bourgeois, capitalist ideology.

These two articles indicated the rise of the second generation. This new generation exhibited the healthy growth of various voices, most in support of continuing the black theological project, but some opposing it as hegemonic and inadequate for the liberation of all African American people. The different voices spoke from different perspectives. The "popular culture" view (i.e., using popular sources to do theology) drew on popular music (such as jazz, rap, and soul), commonsense folk wisdom, and myths of black males. A second view relied heavily on "black poor folk" as the primary sources for doing theology. If black theology relies on the religious experiences of the folk, what do they add to constructing a theology and ethics? Afrocentricity, a third voice, called on black theology and any form of black religious scholarship to replace Europe with Africa as the center of study, worship, and life. In the biblical field,

Afrocentric writers have asked: Where are the white people in the Bible?

A fourth group in the second generation, one that spoke of remaking traditional disciplines, accepted the traditional theological categories but sought to rework them as a source of liberation for the least in society. They raised the interesting challenge of being part of the academy and, at the same time, seeking to subvert or radically transform the academy. A fifth group of writings in the second generation emphasized global connections, calling on black theology to learn from and extend its contributions into the global theological arena. It instructed black theology to join with allies doing African theology and various other forms of black theology throughout the globe. A sixth group of younger scholars fell under the category of "challenging black theology's claims of liberation." They raised questions about so-called positive dimensions of Jesus' suffering for black people. Similarly, challenges were raised pertaining to the enduring suffering of African Americans, which continued even after the civil rights and black power movements. Perhaps Christianity had, indeed, been an opiate for oppressed black people. The final group of second-generation scholars was those who used interdisciplinary approaches, attempting to put black theology in conversation with other bodies of knowledge in order to learn new lessons for today. These scholars have used disciplines like cultural studies and anthropology to critique black theology.

Chapter 3 concluded by exploring four challenges which the second generation faces. These challenges are different from those faced by the first generation of religious scholars, who entered national theological discussions from a position of being connected both to churches and to larger cultural and political movements of African Americans organizing for their freedom. The first challenge of the second generation is to examine, in very creative ways, the critical complexity of black theology and African American religious thought, and to do this it has to maintain awareness that the core of the *gospel message* is a call for a close connection between the Bible and the poor and marginalized in society. Perhaps there are exceptions, but most of the second generation have arrived on the theological scene as a result of this theological claim which was pioneered by first-generation thinkers and many black churches.

Second, there is a danger of forgetting the pains and aspirations of the those in the African American *churches* and *communities*. Black theology emerged in direct response to its connections to black churches and the requirements in the larger civic society. It did not emerge as an isolated intellectual pursuit in and of itself. Theology serves the community and the church. Third, there is a need for more sophisticated *interdisciplinary theoretical frameworks*. Fourth, we need to identify more exactly the location of the pockets of *passionate resistance* in the African American church and broader black experience. If we still believe that Jesus Christ is with the oppressed in their experience of pain and efforts at transformation, then where precisely is this revealed? Fifth, an important critical, long-term conversation needs to start between *womanist and second-generation male* theologians as a way of systematically engaging their commonalities and differences. The goal of this conversation will be the overall health of the church and the community. And sixth, we need to promote and learn from particular *positive local models* of black Christians working on the grassroots level, whether in the form of one church or in the experience of Christian house gatherings.

As discussed in chapter 4, one of the most dynamic developments in the second generation of black theologians was the rise of womanist theologians. First of all, womanist theologians — the self-description of African American female religious scholars and pastors who adopted this title from Alice Walker's vocabulary — describe their unique positive relationship with God. Next, they differentiate themselves from black and white men (due to sexism) and from white women and men (because of racism); they draw out, moreover, their total relationship with God, a connection which cannot separate their race from their gender; in fact, their understanding of method (i.e., how they go about doing their specific type of theology) begins with the idea of a holistic or interrelated approach to doing theology.

Four points were made in reference to their method. First, their holistic method includes relating God to the concerns of all African American women, whose identities are multiple. What is the relation between God and a heterosexual woman's blackness and gender? What does it mean to be black, female, and lesbian? How does the divine reveal the divine self to black working-class women? Is there a sacred interaction between African American women and nature?

Second, a holistic approach also pertains to black women's different ways of being human (e.g., spiritual, religious, cultural, sociological, political, economic, linguistic, and aesthetic). Third, because they relate to God with multiple identities and because they experience diverse ways of being human, womanists' holistic method for doing theology includes the use of various disciplines of knowledge (e.g., anthropology, literary studies, and political economy). These ways of knowing help African American women to better analyze who they are and how they were created. This knowledge aids their healthy ties to God and what God has called them to do. In addition, it is from understanding their identities and human nature that womanists draw their creative use of sources of divine revelation.

Fourth, womanist theologians and ethicists claim universal implications of their method of doing theology. Because they examine how faith and practice connect to women, they speak to all women; the exploration of racial oppression includes all impacted by white racism; the economic issue of class touches all affected by economic exploitation; analysis of sexual orientation and the revelation of God underscore the reality that faith issues are not just for black lesbians, but all lesbian and gay faith communities; and a theological engagement with ecology impacts not only all of humanity but nature as well. Similarly, womanists accept the universal dimension of their theology and ethics because of their explicit embracing of the spiritual and material well-being of the black men and black children in their lives.

Chapter 5 discussed the globalization of black theology. From its beginning, black theology and African American clergy have extended their hands to the international movements of diverse liberation theologies. This natural dynamic arose from the historical, cultural, and religious interchange between African Americans and Africa, an interchange based primarily on black Americans' historical links to Africa but also based, theologically speaking, on a recurring theme in black history, a theme articulated in Ps. 68:31 — "Princes shall come out of Egypt and Ethiopia shall soon stretch forth her hand unto God." In the more immediate context of the 1950s and 1960s, both Martin King Jr. and Malcolm X touched on the international ties between black Americans' efforts at justice and the African independence movements. This backdrop, coupled with black theologians' and African Americans' racial consciousness of their own fate as it linked to European racial colonialism on the Continent, cemented a belief in a theological union between dark peoples on both sides of the Atlantic.

Black theology's first introduction to Third World theologies occurred when the National Committee of Negro Churchmen sent delegates to the 1969 assembly of the All Africa Conference of Churches. Since that time, black American theologians have maintained consistent dialogue with African religious scholars and church leaders. Agreeing with African American religious scholars, black South African theologians and a few in Cameroon have agreed on the political thrust of the gospel and, therefore, on a need for an explicit black theology accenting liberation from political systems of white supremacy. However, the majority of African theologians have emphasized culture and faith — the need to reinterpret Christianity within the context of indigenous cultures and religions of African peoples.

From the first encounter of U.S. black theology of liberation with Latin American liberation theology, which occurred at a May 1973 conference organized by the World Council of Churches, Latin American theologians have asserted strongly that the liberation offered by Jesus Christ has to do specifically with the working class, thus the vital necessity of a political class analysis in matters of faith and practice. In contrast, American black theologians have held fast to the connection of race and God's divine revelation, and thus they call for a sophisticated racial analysis in the doing of theology in church and society. Over the years, both have appreciated and accepted the importance of race and class in defining Jesus Christ's presence with the poor. Still, each enters theology from its own historical and contemporary experiences of race and class.

When U.S. black theology first met Asian theologies, particularly dialogue with Korean Japanese Christians in Japan in May 1975, an immediate solidarity flourished. This was due to Asia's many-sided approach to theology. Such a comprehensive approach to faith included a deep appreciation for racial affirmation, cultural contributions, economic exploitation, and sociological and political oppression.

Today, the Ecumenical Association of Third World Theologians is the only dialogue organization of liberation theologians from Africa, Asia, the Caribbean, Latin America, the Pacific Islands, and U.S. minorities. Black theologians from the United States are welcomed fully in this global gathering.[1] Various agreements exist among the theologians in this worldwide liberation theology movement. (1) God reveals God's self among the poor in their efforts toward full humanity. (2) The vocation of the church and the theologian is to side with the plight and prospects of the poor. (3) Theology begins first with a faith commitment; the second step is academic reflection on this practice. (4) With the poor, liberation theology rereads the Bible and discovers a thread of divine will and activity focused on liberation. (5) Liberation theology takes seriously the importance of spiritual development, prayer, and worship. (6) All theologies are contextual, arising out of specific communities and peoples. In a related manner, humans, not God, do theology, and therefore the poor — not simply mainstream academic scholars — are entitled to do theology. (7) Liberation theologians throughout the globe believe that the good news of love, liberation, and salvation is offered to all of humanity.

Challenges for Black Theology Today

The primary question for this book has been: What does it mean to be black and Christian? The answer offered has been that to be black and Christian means to have faith and a practice which experience God as a presence and reality of liberation for the least in the African American community. Consequently, the purpose of a black theology of liberation is to work with the church and community to see God's will of liberation through Jesus Christ as similar to black folk's attempts at liberation. The June 13, 1969, theological statement of the National Committee of Black Churchmen still applies today. It offered the following definition:

> Black Theology is a theology of black liberation. It seeks to plumb the black condition in the light of God's revelation in Jesus Christ, so that the black community can see that the gospel is commensurate with the achievement of black humanity.[2]

This divine calling is to the individual Christian, the church, and the larger African American community. Moreover, such a vocation covers every level of experience — the spiritual and the material, the individual and the group, the church and outside the church, and the black community and beyond that one unique reality. Thus black theology calls on us to use our faith and witness in all aspects of the African American experience. It is a belief that God is present and liberates all parts of what it means to be black in the world. One helpful way of detecting God's presence of liberation (i.e., the signs of the times) is to view reality as both internal and external. There exist external pressures on the entire African American community — racist practices, economic exploitation, and cultural exclusion. At the same time, additional demonic forces tear away at the liberation possibilities within the community. In other words, demonic forces wage war against God's will of liberation for the poor and the oppressed both outside and inside the African American context. Within the framework of the community, the struggle against powers of slavery and for powers of liberation takes place. Black theology has to pursue liberation on various levels.

First, we have to engage the individual on the spiritual level, which includes gaining clarity about God's call of liberation for each African American person. This will entail overcoming internal demonic presences which derail us from our ability to hear, understand, and carry out the divine will of liberation. Biblical stories and psychotherapy teach us that our full potential as free individuals capable of aiding in the liberation of others is greatly damaged due to scars, wounds, and negative issues that have not been resolved from harmful childhood and adult experiences. This covers many problems — low self-esteem, sexual abuse of children, children in the care of alcoholic adults, domestic violence, and different ways that we are addicted to being dependent on other people or other things in our environment. We cannot reach our full liberated potential in relation to community if these psychological and emotional obstacles continue to make us do negative things to ourselves and to others.

Furthermore, if we do not pay attention to these negative feelings and actions, we then pass them on to our children and impact our loved ones, our colleagues, and others with whom we come in contact. Moreover, those who have power project the scars of their childhood onto society and the world. It is extremely difficult to be a productive human being when one walks around filled with negative thoughts and feelings.

Engagement with the process of healing requires, among other things, both individual and group processes. On the individual level, we need to practice daily spiritual disciplines which could include prayer, Bible study, and meditation over healing and recovery. At the group level, the black church is known for its ministry of conversion and healing. But the healing cannot simply be "one size fits all." It has to speak to the specific kinds of pains of particular individuals. Because one of the strong points of black church ministry has been its emphasis on conversion of the spirit, the African American church is very ably equipped to take on this specific challenge. Coupled with involvement in the church, we need to devise adequate healing processes, such as attending professional group and individual sessions, in addition to appropriate 12-step programs. What is at stake is God's will for liberation of all humanity, especially the least in society. Because black theology calls the African American church to theological accountability to this calling, each individual has to practice spiritual liberation with him- or herself and in community.

Second, we have to improve gender relations in the African American church and in black theology. Perhaps one of the hardest challenges to liberation which faces the African American church is the relation between men and women. If Christian liberation means anything, it, at the very least, suggests that the African American church should work with poor black women so that they can reach their full humanity. There should not be any automatic roles that men occupy because such specifying of roles denies the full humanity of women and stifles the creativity of all members of the body of Christ and the black community. An enlarged freedom and humanity call for a reexamination of women's roles in the church. Women need to be able to choose new styles of church leadership and to become pastors of black churches. If African American women (the majority of whom are poor and working-class) make up at least 70 percent of the congregations, why is it that they do not make up 70 percent of the black pastors? Similarly, women should have the option of choosing which roles they desire in the family; this is an important issue for black churches concerned about family values. Also, the church should encourage black women, especially poor and working women, to move into leadership positions in the broader society of education, corporate wealth, and politics.

Further, the church should encourage women to love themselves more. The more they take care of themselves and are not servants to or dependent on men, the more they will be able to develop more healthy relations. Most of the time, it is assumed that whatever happens, the black woman will be there to take care of the situation, or clean up after everyone else, or sacrifice her life, body, health, pleasures, job, and ideas in order for husbands, children, or the church to feel better. In the worst situation, African American women have had to play the role of the Mule for the church, for the rest of the black community, and for white people. Poor black women have to develop increased values of self-love and independence. It is hypocritical for people to sing gospel and spiritual songs about loving Jesus when they do not love themselves. True love for Jesus is expressed in self-love.

In addition to the woman's part of the gender relationship, black men share an obligation for self-inspection. It entails examining the specific question, What does it mean to be a black man and Christian? Part of the response includes a redefinition of maleness or manhood. Unfortunately today, there are privileges that African American men enjoy simply because of their gender. The black church cannot continue to proclaim that we are all created equal by God when black women in the church, the society, and at home are relegated to a secondary and subservient status. Furthermore, the black church loses all of its legitimacy when it critiques white racism as a sin but participates in attitudes and structures of patriarchy.

Therefore, to be a new man demands that we raise some hard questions. What do black churchmen do to and for their wives and significant others? How do they raise their children? What negative beliefs and practices do they bring into their families, churches, and communities which they imitate from the larger society of cut-throat competition? Why are domestic violence, wife-battering, various addictions, and child abuse such taboo topics in black churches? How do African American male Christians handle conflict, stress, anger, forms of self-hatred, despair, joy, love, faith, and other challenges as they relate to being a black man in the United States?

From a more positive perspective, the redefinition of manhood has to examine more closely what following the will of God means on an immediate and personal level. If liberation is the key to God's will for the church and theology, then positioning God's liberation at the center of a man's life would become a daily practice. In other words, the love of liberation would begin within the self (i.e., the desire to do God's will by loving oneself) and would move outward toward significant others (i.e., compassion for the well-being of loved ones), the church and the community (i.e., healthy relations to aid the least in society), and all of nature (i.e., appreciating the interconnection between humanity and all of creation). In sum, a redefinition of black manhood comprises the God of liberation being at the center of the individual's daily life and the embodiment of new spiritual and practical traits — such as, embracing feelings and thinking, tears and laughter, accountability and responsibility, and partnership and equality.

Third, in addition to the individual spiritual level and gender relations, to be black and Christian means bringing the gospel of liberation to the issue of sexual orientation as it relates to the African American church and black theology. One of the greatest points of unity that most black heterosexual Christians have is their agreement to oppress and discriminate against African American lesbians and gays in the church, the family, and the community. Black heterosexuals have a privilege over black homosexuals. Though black heterosexuals suffer from class exploitation, racial oppression, and, in the case of black women, male supremacy, they still perpetuate the subordination of lesbians and gays. African American heterosexual Christians tragically continue a system of discrimination against lesbians and gays by using some of the same arguments that whites have used against blacks, and men have employed against women.

The Bible is brought into the conversation as a justification to hold black lesbians and gays down. Yet it is a problem when African American churches interpret the Bible as wrong when it calls on slaves to obey their masters and women to obey men, and then the black church interprets the Bible as saying homosexuals cannot be saved unless they become heterosexuals. A related argument accuses lesbians and gays of destroying the black family. This claim presupposes the traditional notion of family where the patriarch rules and the woman has his children; man is still the center and authority of the family. However, the black church and community have always defined their own experience of being a family in America. This method of self-definition could expand the notion of family so that it includes lesbians and gays, many of whom are struggling to build stable families and raise their children. To be consistent in its faith in a Christianity for all people, the church should expand its notion of family so that homosexuals, especially poor African American lesbians and gays, can achieve their full humanity.

Fourth, to aid the African American church in its vocational response to the question of being black and Christian, black theology continues to encourage the church to affirm black beauty as reflecting the image of God. Such an affirmation promotes the racial and cultural contributions of poor and working people, in particular. The more the church blesses the healthy cultural gifts of all parts of the community, the more it will be practicing its belief that all citizens, even the least in its own community, have the divine creativity of liberation within them. This affirmation of race and culture also encourages the self-esteem of the least in the community and helps make them feel part of the larger society. Thus they have the potential to become more loyal and productive citizens of a society prioritizing liberation and full humanity for all.

The theological vocation of revealing black as beautiful entails a cultural rebirth. To this end, black theology needs to work with churches in the development of church education and curricula. A specific ongoing project should be the removal of all white pictures of Jesus from African American churches and homes. This has several implications. (*a*) The ongoing subservience to European models of Jesus damages the psychological health of blacks, who face racism in a society where the overwhelming majority of authority figures and people with power are white. (*b*) Many black biblical scholars assert that Jesus was of African descent, with some Asian lineage. In fact, some suggest that most whites in the Bible are colonial occupiers from Rome. Thus they have asked the question: Where are the white characters in the Bible? And, (*c*) the removal of white portraits of Jesus signifies a theological question. Why is it that people of African descent worship a white divinity if they believe they are made in God's image?

Fifth, black theology interprets the church's accountability to the vocation of God's will of liberation as involvement in various macro and structural arenas. The wealth of the United States remains in the hands of a few white families who own and control industries, capital, land, technology, and resources. However, God has created wealth for all to own and use equally. In this sense, no one elite group should monopolize any parts of creation. Indeed, we are all stewards of that which belongs to God. As equal stewards, we should all have equal and collective access to the ownership of wealth and the distribution of the fruits of this wealth. Private ownership of resources structurally forbids the democratization, equalization, and collectivization of stewardship. This remains one of the biggest affronts against God's gift to all humanity. Furthermore, such a systemic arrangement perpetually maintains and creates a pyramidlike social relation of greed and poverty.

Further, the vocation of liberation and full humanity for the least in the society urges the church to engage in politics and public policy. If the vocation of the black church touches on justice for the oppressed, then the church has to take its faith into the public realm of politics. Politics should focus upon the codification of laws and acceptable ways for citizens to interact based on the well-being of the least in society. Public policy should reflect this touchstone criterion and starting point. Similarly, elected offices not only should reflect this criterion but also should be occupied by a greater proportion of poor and oppressed people themselves. In this way, politics and public policy would prioritize the health of communities facing the destruction of black children and youth, wholesale drug ownership and distribution, the discarding of the African American elderly, crime, and an unjust legal system producing a major disproportion of black people in prisons. Politics and public policy would also emphasize basic survival needs of poor people — such as equal access to and preparation for all jobs; food; shelter; clothing; children's education; universal health insurance; and equal access to leisure activities.

To begin work on these macro issues, black theology and black churches could utilize a host of practical strategies of pressure and implementation, including boycotts, labor struggles, sit-ins, mass demonstrations, voting, setting up picket lines, and petition drives.

Black theology should begin with the few prophetic churches, church-related institutions, and other institutions that are strug-

gling to offer leadership in African American communities and
that are taking seriously a vocational calling to empower poor
and other victims of dehumanizing internal and external structures of pain and sin. Such a beginning reaches out to embrace
blacks in the church pews, the oppressed themselves, pastors,
and professors. This organization would have several foundational goals: (1) to further develop black theology for and in
the black churches; there is a need for more theoretical work
to clarify the intellectual nature of the challenges today; (2) to
mobilize churches and the community to implement radical political, cultural, and economic activities in the public arena;
(3) to enhance the spiritual well-being and diverse ways of
becoming a full human being within the African American community; (4) to cultivate spiritual humility through self-criticism
of black theology and the black church based on the norm of
freedom for oppressed African Americans; and (5) to extend
hands to global allies, particularly in Africa, those of African descent around the globe, and liberation theologies in the
Third World.

In a word, an introduction to a black theology of liberation
draws us into increased intellectual pursuits and a more practical faith grounded in justice. However, this is not merely a
subjective justice, but a faith and vision to work with the divine
will of liberation. The God of freedom, Jesus Christ the liberator, and the empowering Holy Spirit are manifest in what it
means to be black and Christian today. The ultimate challenge
to realize the full humanity of all — anchored in a focus on the
least in the African American community — is the development
of a way of being black in the world such that we produce a
more comprehensive faith and practice for ourselves and for our
children. The Spirit of hope, determination, and liberation continues to move African Americans. This world didn't make that
Spirit, and this world can't take it away.

Notes

Introduction

1. W. E. B. Du Bois, *The Souls of Black Folk* (Greenwich, Conn.: Fawcett, 1968), 23.

2. See Lewis R. Gordon's insightful theoretical development of the notion of antiblack racism in his *Bad Faith and Antiblack Racism* (Atlantic Highlands, N.J.: Humanities Press, 1995).

3. Du Bois, *Souls of Black Folk,* and his *The Gift of Black Folk: The Negroes in the Making of America* (New York: Washington Square Press, 1970).

4. Orbis Books, Maryknoll, N.Y., has an extensive list of writings by and about liberation theologians around the world. Representatives of black theology from throughout the globe held their first worldwide conference in South Africa in August 1993. The conference was sponsored by the Ecumenical Association of Third World Theologians.

5. For different interpretations of the development of black theology, see Gayraud S. Wilmore, general introduction to *Black Theology: A Documentary History, 1966–1979,* ed. James H. Cone and Gayraud S. Wilmore (Maryknoll, N.Y.: Orbis Books, 1979); idem, general introduction to *Black Theology: A Documentary History, Volume One, 1966–1979,* ed. James H. Cone and Gayraud S. Wilmore (Maryknoll, N.Y.: Orbis Books, 1993); James H. Cone, *For My People: Black Theology and the Black Church* (Maryknoll, N.Y.: Orbis Books, 1984), chap. 1; and Dwight N. Hopkins, introduction to *Cut Loose Your Stammering Tongue: Black Theology in the Slave Narratives,* ed. Dwight N. Hopkins and George C. L. Cummings (Maryknoll, N.Y.: Orbis Books, 1991).

6. See "Black Power: Statement by the National Committee of Negro Churchmen," in Wilmore and Cone, *Black Theology, 1966–79.*

7. James H. Cone, *Black Theology and Black Power* (New York: Seabury Press, 1969); rev. ed., Maryknoll, N.Y.: Orbis Books, 1998.

8. See Wilmore, general introduction (1979), 5.

1. The Development of Black Theology

1. For theological interpretations of the Invisible Institution, see Dwight N. Hopkins and George C. L. Cummings, eds., *Cut Loose Your Stammering Tongue: Black Theology in the Slave Narratives* (Maryknoll, N.Y.: Orbis Books, 1991).

2. For example: talking to ancestors who were dead, putting the belongings of the dead person on her or his grave, believing that religion was not private but part of everyday public and private life, the act of shouting while worshiping, respect for elders, and the key role of the extended family.

3. John S. Mbiti, *African Religions and Philosophy* (Garden City, N.Y.: Anchor Books, 1970), 37.

4. See Kofi Asare Opoku, *West African Traditional Religion* (Accra, Ghana: FEP International Private Limited, 1978), 9–10; and Philip D. Curtin, ed., *Africa Remembered: Narratives by West Africans from the Era of the Slave Trade* (Madison: University of Wisconsin Press, 1968), 274.

5. Curtin, *Africa Remembered*, 78.

6. See John S. Mbiti, *Introduction to African Religion* (Portsmouth, N.H.: Heinemann Educational Books, 1991), 29; and John S. Pobee, *Toward an African Theology* (Nashville: Abingdon, 1979), 44.

7. John S. Mbiti, *Concepts of God in Africa* (London: SPCK, 1979), 120–21.

8. Quoted in George P. Rawick, ed., *The American Slave: A Composite Autobiography,* vol. 19, *God Struck Me Dead* (Westport, Conn.: Greenwood Publishing Company, 1977), 124–25.

9. Quoted in Charles L. Perdue Jr., ed., *Weevils in the Wheat: Interviews with Virginia Ex-Slaves* (Bloomington: Indiana University Press, 1980), 126.

10. "The Narrative of Lunsford Lane," in *Five Slave Narratives,* ed. William Loren Katz (New York: Arno Press, 1968), 20.

11. "A Slave Girl's Story, Being an Autobiography of Kate Drumgoold," in *Six Women's Slave Narratives,* ed. William L. Andrews (New York: Oxford University Press, 1988), 3.

12. Ibid., 30.

13. Joseph R. Washington Jr., *Black Religion: The Negro and Christianity in the United States* (1964; reprint, Lanham, Md.: University Press of America, 1984), 22.

14. Ibid., 23.

15. Ibid., 38–39.

16. Ibid., 255.

17. See David J. Garrow, *Bearing the Cross: Martin Luther King, Jr., and the Southern Christian Leadership Conference* (New York: Vintage

Books, 1986); and Taylor Branch, *Parting the Waters: America in the King Years, 1954–63* (New York: Simon and Schuster, 1988).

18. Robert L. Allen, *Black Awakening in Capitalist America* (Garden City, N.Y.: Anchor Books, 1970), 26–27; Benjamin Quarles, *The Negro in the Making of America* (New York: Macmillan, 1969), 262, 272–73; Nathan Wright Jr., "The Crisis Which Bred Black Power," in *The Black Power Revolt,* ed. Floyd B. Barbour (Boston: Beacon Press, 1968), 104–8; and John Hope Franklin, *From Slavery to Freedom: A History of Negro Americans,* 5th ed. (New York: Alfred A. Knopf, 1980), 479–80.

19. Allen J. Matusow, "From Civil Rights to Black Power: The Case of SNCC, 1960–1966," in *Twentieth Century America,* ed. Barton J. Bernstein and Allen J. Matusow (New York: Harcourt, Brace and World, 1969), 543; see also Clayborne Carson, *In Struggle: SNCC and the Black Awakening of the 1960s* (Cambridge, Mass.: Harvard University Press, 1982); Harvard Sitkoff, *The Struggle for Black Equality, 1954–1980* (New York: Hill and Wang, 1981), 184–85; John Oliver Killens, *Black Man's Burden* (New York: Simon and Schuster, 1965), chap. 1; and Juan Williams, *Eyes on the Prize: America's Civil Rights Years, 1954–1965* (New York: Viking, 1987), 243–49.

20. See Sitkoff, *Struggle,* 114–17, 124; also see, Robert H. Brisbane, *Black Activism: Racial Revolution in the United States, 1954–1970* (Valley Forge, Pa.: Judson Press, 1974), 80–81; and Matusow, "Civil Rights," 537.

21. See Malcolm X, *The Autobiography of Malcolm X* (New York: Grove Press, 1966).

22. The following are useful works on the origin and concerns of the NCNC-NCBC: Gayraud S. Wilmore and James H. Cone, eds., *Black Theology: A Documentary History, 1966–1979* (Maryknoll, N.Y.: Orbis Books, 1979); idem, eds., *Black Theology: A Documentary History, 1980–1992* (Maryknoll, N.Y.: Orbis Books, 1993); Gayraud S. Wilmore, *Black Religion and Black Radicalism,* 3d, rev. ed. (Maryknoll, N.Y.: Orbis Books, 1998); James H. Cone, *For My People: Black Theology and the Black Church* (Maryknoll, N.Y.: Orbis Books, 1984); Grant S. Schockley, "Ultimatum and Hope, the Black Churchmen's Convocation: An Interpretation," *Christian Century,* February 12, 1969, 217–19; Leon W. Watts II, "The National Committee of Black Churchmen," *Christian Century,* November 2, 1970, and November 16, 1970; Alex Poinsett, "The Black Power Revolt in White Churches," *Ebony* (September 1968): 63–68; see also *Time,* November 15, 1968, 78, and *Look,* January 7, 1969, 84–85.

23. Gayraud S. Wilmore, "Appendix D: The Theological Commission Project of the National Committee of Negro Churchmen, Fall 1968," in

Christian Faith in Black and White, ed. Warner R. Traynham (Wakefield, Mass.: Parameter Press, 1973), 84.

24. On the civil rights movement, see Sitkoff, *Struggle;* Brisbane, *Black Activism,* chaps. 1–4; Lerone Bennett Jr., *Before the Mayflower: A History of Black America* (Chicago: Johnson, 1987); Franklin, *From Slavery to Freedom;* and Williams, *Eyes on the Prize.*

25. From my March 17, 1987, interview with Rev. Dr. Calvin B. Marshall.

26. From my March 23, 1987, interview with Reverend Leon W. Watts II. Both Marshall (see previous note) and Watts are members of the African Methodist Episcopal Zion Church, one of the historic black denominations.

27. James H. Cone, *Black Theology and Black Power* (New York: Seabury Press, 1969); reprinted Maryknoll, N.Y.: Orbis Books, 1997.

2. The First Generation

1. Aimé Césaire, a Martinican poet and politician, created the term "Negritude," with its meaning of "blackness," in the early 1930s. Leopold Senghor, however, defined and refined the ideology of Negritude. See Senghor, *Liberté I: Negritude et humanisme* (Paris, 1964).

2. See Steve Biko, "The Definitions of Black Consciousness," in *Steve Biko: I Write What I Like* (San Francisco: Harper and Row, 1986), 49.

3. Albert Cleage labels his "very good friend Dr. James H. Cone" black people's "apostle to the Gentiles," because Cone drags "white Christians as far as they are able to go (and then some) in interpreting Black theology within the established framework which they can accept and understand" (Cleage, *Black Christian Nationalism* [New York: William Morrow, 1972], xvii, n.).

4. See James H. Cone, *Black Theology and Black Power* (New York: Seabury Press, 1969), 82–90; reprint: Maryknoll, N.Y: Orbis Books, 1997; idem, introduction to *Black Theology: A Documentary History, 1966–1979,* ed. Gayraud S. Wilmore and James H. Cone (Maryknoll, N.Y.: Orbis Books, 1979), 135–43; and idem, *My Soul Looks Back* (Nashville: Abingdon, 1982), chap. 2.

5. James H. Cone, "Black Power, Black Theology, and the Study of Theology and Ethics," *Theological Education* (spring 1970): 209.

6. From my March 31, 1987, interview with James H. Cone.

7. Regarding the "nonperson" comment, see Cone, *Black Theology and Black Power,* 11; see ibid., 40–41, for Cone's view on "the white structure of this American society."

8. See James H. Cone, "Freedom, History, and Hope," *Journal of the Interdenominational Theological Center* 1, no. 1 (fall 1973): 56; and idem, *Black Theology and Black Power,* 43.

9. Cone, "Black Theology and Black Liberation," *Christian Century,* September 16, 1970, 1086–87; and idem, *Black Theology and Black Power,* 36–37.

10. Cone, *Black Theology and Black Power,* 35, 38, and 120; see also his *A Black Theology of Liberation,* 2d ed. (Maryknoll, N.Y.: Orbis Books, 1986), 120–21; the latter work was also reprinted by Orbis Books in a twentieth-anniversary edition in 1990.

11. Actually, Cone dismisses two members of the black theological political trend: J. Deotis Roberts and Albert Cleage. In 1974 Roberts stated: "For blacks, Jesus is understood in a psychocultural sense. He leads us to a new self-understanding. He helps us to overcome the identity crisis triggered by white oppression of blacks" (Roberts, *A Black Political Theology* [Philadelphia: Westminster Press, 1974], 137). In 1968, Cleage wrote: "We are convinced, upon the basis of our knowledge and historical study of all the facts, that Jesus was born to a black Mary, that Jesus, the Messiah, was a black man" (Cleage, *The Black Messiah* [New York: Sheed and Ward, 1968], 85). See the next note for information on Cone's rebuttal of these positions.

12. James H. Cone, *God of the Oppressed* (New York: Seabury Press, 1975), 135–37; rev. ed.: Maryknoll, N.Y.: Orbis Books, 1987; on p. 136 of the original edition of the work, Cone opposes Roberts's notion of psychocultural. "Christ," Cone claims, "is black, therefore, not because of some cultural or psychological need of black people, but because and only because Christ really enters into our world where the poor, the despised, and the black are." In *For My People* (Maryknoll, N.Y.: Orbis Books, 1984), Cone attacks Cleage's "black Messiah" christology for "distorting history and the Christian gospel" (36).

13. Cone, *Black Theology of Liberation,* 110–24.

14. Cone, *Black Theology and Black Power,* 35, 42–43; see also idem, *Black Theology of Liberation,* 6.

15. See Cone's introduction to *Black Theology and Black Power.*

16. Ibid., 145; James H. Cone, "Toward a Black Theology," *Ebony* 25, no. 10 (August 1970): 114. Aiming to lay out some of the terms of reconciliation, Cone combats white people's seemingly inevitable practice of setting the terms in black-white encounters. Cone points out that if power were redistributed, then white inclination to abusive authority over blacks would lack the potency to implement itself. Cone also fights for the right of the oppressed community to self-determination when dealing with oppressors.

17. See James H. Cone, "Theological Reflections on Reconciliation," *Christianity and Crisis,* January 22, 1973, 307–8; idem, *God of the Oppressed,* 235–46; and idem, *Black Theology and Black Power,* 150–51.

18. J. Deotis Roberts, *Faith and Reason: A Comparative Study of Pascal, Bergson, and James* (Boston: Christopher Publishers House, 1962); idem, *From Puritanism to Platonism in Seventeenth Century England* (The Hague: Martinus Nijhoff, 1968).

19. J. Deotis Roberts, *Liberation and Reconciliation* (Philadelphia: Westminster Press, 1971), 34; rev. ed.: Maryknoll, N.Y.: Orbis Books, 1994. Cleage and Cone were the two members of the group who published books prior to Roberts's.

20. Roberts, *Black Political Theology.*

21. Roberts, *Liberation and Reconciliation,* 34; see also idem, *Black Political Theology,* 26.

22. Roberts, *Liberation and Reconciliation,* 28.

23. These comments are from my March 19, 1987, interview with him; for other references to his "balance" approach, see Roberts, *Liberation and Reconciliation,* 13. For his definition of theology, see "Black Theology in the Making," *Review and Expositor* 70 (1973): 321. On his interpretation of "Christian," see his "Black Theology in Faith and Ethics," in *Black Theology Today: Liberation and Contextualization* (New York: Mellen Press, 1983), 58; idem, "Black Liberation Theism," *Journal of Religious Thought* 33, no. 1 (spring–summer 1976): 33; and idem, "The Roots of Black Theology: An Historic Perspective," in *Black Theology Today,* 83. For black theology as "inner-city" theology, examine his *Black Political Theology,* 115.

24. Roberts, *Liberation and Reconciliation,* 43.

25. Roberts, "Black Theology in Faith and Ethics," 65, and idem, *Liberation and Reconciliation,* 26. He also writes: "I stand somewhere between the generations — that is, on the boundary between the black militants and the old-fashioned civil rights integrationists, and also between the 'by whatever means necessary' ethicists and the view that liberation and reconciliation must be considered at the same time and in relation to each other" (*Liberation and Reconciliation,* 13).

26. For Roberts's claims regarding the black Messiah and the colorless Christ and his opinions on liberation and reconciliation, see his *Liberation and Reconciliation,* chap. 6, and *Black Political Theology,* chap. 5.

27. Gayraud S. Wilmore, *Black Religion and Black Radicalism* (Maryknoll, N.Y.: Orbis Books, 1972); 3d rev. ed.: Maryknoll, N.Y.: Orbis Books, 1998.

28. Wilmore and Cone, *Black Theology, 1966–1979;* idem, eds., *Black*

Theology: A Documentary History, 1980–1992 (Maryknoll, N.Y.: Orbis Books, 1993).

29. From my February 19, 1987, interview with Wilmore.

30. See Wilmore, *Black Religion and Black Radicalism,* 218–19.

31. Gayraud S. Wilmore, "Black Theology: Its Significance for Christian Mission Today," *International Review of Mission* 63, no. 250 (April 1974): 214.

32. Wilmore, *Black Religion and Black Radicalism,* 237.

33. Ibid., 234–41.

34. Ibid., 222.

35. Wilmore's views and quotes on Africanisms come from my February 19, 1987, interview with him; see also *Black Religion and Black Radicalism,* 239; and his "Reinterpretation in Black Church History," *Chicago Theological Seminary Register* (winter 1983): 29.

36. Wilmore, *Black Religion and Black Radicalism,* 219.

37. Wilmore, "Black Theology: Its Significance," 215.

38. Gayraud S. Wilmore, "Spirituality and Social Transformation as the Vocation of the Black Church," in *Churches in Struggle: Liberation Theologies and Social Transformation in North America,* ed. William Tabb (New York: Monthly Review Press, 1986), 240–41.

39. From my February 19, 1987, interview with Wilmore. In "Spirituality and Social Transformation," he writes: "To speak of the mission and strategy of the black church as the cultural rather than political is not to deny the political, but to subsume it in a larger context; and it is precisely in such a context that we can see how the spiritual dimension of life impinges upon the problems and possibilities of social transformation. This means that we intend to encompass the entire scale of perceptions, meanings, values, behavioral patterns, etc., all integrated in that system of symbols we call culture,...and take passionate actions on the basis of such conceptions" (248).

40. Charles H. Long, "The West African High God: History and Religious Experience," *History of Religions* 3, no. 2 (winter 1964): 331.

41. Charles H. Long, *Significations* (Philadelphia: Fortress Press, 1986), 7. In my February 21, 1987, interview with him, Long commented: out of religion "all the other languages come; all of it comes from this attempt to orient yourself in your time and space. Religion is produced out of the culture.... Given all that, and for black theology to come along and then narrow [religious language] all down again."

42. Interview of February 21, 1987.

43. Interview of February 21, 1987; see also Charles H. Long, "Freedom, Otherness, and Religion: Theologies Opaque," *Chicago Theological Seminary Register* (winter 1983): 20–22.

44. Interview of February 21, 1987.

45. Long, "Perspectives for a Study of Afro-American Religion in the United States," *History of Religions* 11, no. 1 (August 1971): 55.

46. Interview of February 21, 1987.

47. Long, "Perspectives," 59–62. From his three sections I deduce four sources. Unless indicated otherwise, quotations in this section come from this article.

48. For his views and suggestions on Africanism, see Charles H. Long, "A New Look at American Religion," *Anglican Theological Review* (July 1973): 122; and idem, "Perspectives," 57–59.

49. Long, *Significations*, 170. Long also elaborated similar points in my interview with him.

50. Long, *Significations*, 106.

51. Charles H. Long, "The Black Reality: Toward a Theology of Freedom," *Criterion* 8, no. 2 (spring–summer 1969): 6. Long points out the possibility of liberation for the larger humanity coming through the "otherness" in the black community.

52. Charles H. Long, "Structural Similarities and Dissimilarities in Black and African Theologies," *Journal of Religious Thought* 32, no. 2 (fall–winter 1975): 16–17.

53. Ibid., 24.

54. Charles H. Long, "New Space, New Time: Disjunctions and Context for New World Religions," *Criterion* (winter 1985): 7.

3. The Second Generation

1. The most recent edition of Cone's book is *Black Theology and Black Power* (Maryknoll, N.Y.: Orbis Books, 1997). On the NCNC and the origin and development of black theology, see James H. Cone, *For My People: Black Theology and the Black Church* (Maryknoll, N.Y.: Orbis Books, 1984); Gayraud S. Wilmore, *Black Religion and Black Radicalism* (Maryknoll, N.Y.: Orbis Books, 1998); Gayraud S. Wilmore and James H. Cone, eds., *Black Theology: A Documentary History, 1966–1979* (Maryknoll, N.Y.: Orbis Books, 1979); Dwight N. Hopkins, *Black Theology USA and South Africa: Politics, Culture, and Liberation* (Maryknoll, N.Y.: Orbis Books, 1989); and Dwight N. Hopkins and George C. L. Cummings, eds., *Cut Loose Your Stammering Tongue: Black Theology in the Slave Narratives* (Maryknoll, N.Y.: Orbis Books, 1991). See also n. 22, chap. 1, above.

The other persons usually mentioned as being part of the first generation are: Vincent Harding, J. Deotis Roberts, Charles H. Long, Major J.

Jones, William R. Jones, Preston Williams, Charles Shelby Rooks, Cecil Cone, Joseph Washington, Carlton L. Lee, Albert Cleage, Charles Copher, and Henry Mitchell. For the historical roles of first-generation participants, their similarities and differences, see Cone's *For My People*.

2. Both articles appear in Wilmore and Cone, *Black Theology, 1966–1979;* Grant's is on pp. 418–33, and West's is on pp. 552–67. The first and second generations contain African Americans trained in diverse disciplines. My use of the term "black theology" is meant to encompass the broad area of African American religious thought.

3. Katie G. Cannon's *Black Womanist Ethics* (Atlanta: Scholars Press, 1988); Renita J. Weems, *Just a Sister Away: A Womanist Vision of Women's Relationships in the Bible* (San Diego: LuraMedia, 1988); and Jacquelyn Grant, *White Women's Christ and Black Women's Jesus* (Atlanta: Scholars Press, 1989).

Other representative, but not exhaustive, womanist voices are: Kelly Brown Douglas, Emilie M. Townes, Jualynne Dodson, Jamie Phelps, Clarice Martin, Cheryl Townsend Gilkes, Cheryl Sanders, Shawn Copeland, Linda E. Thomas, Cheryl Kirk-Duggan, Karen Baker-Fletcher, and Diana L. Hayes. Hayes adds the importance of Roman Catholic womanist thought. See her *Hagar's Daughters: Womanist Ways of Being in the World* (New York: Paulist Press, 1995); and idem, *And Still We Rise: An Introduction to Black Liberation Theology* (New York: Paulist Press, 1996).

4. Delores S. Williams's "Black Women's Literature and the Task of Feminist Theology" is found in *Immaculate and Powerful: The Female in Sacred Image and Social Reality,* ed. Clarissa W. Atkinson, Constance H. Buchanan, and Margaret R. Miles (Boston: Beacon Press, 1985), 88–110; her "Womanist Theology: Black Women's Voices" is found in *Christianity and Crisis* 47, March 2, 1987.

5. Delores S. Williams, *Sisters in the Wilderness: The Challenge of Womanist God-Talk* (Maryknoll, N.Y.: Orbis Books, 1993).

6. In *Journal of Feminist Studies in Religion* 5 (Fall 1989). In addition to this journal, womanist articles appear in the *Journal of Religious Thought.*

7. For nuanced theoretical conversations about popular culture, see John Storey, *An Introductory Guide to Cultural Theory and Popular Culture* (Athens: University of Georgia Press, 1993); and Chandra Mukerji and Michael Schudson, eds., *Rethinking Popular Culture: Contemporary Perspectives in Cultural Studies* (Berkeley: University of California Press, 1991).

8. Jon Michael Spencer, preface to *The Theology of American Popular*

Music, a special issue of *Black Sacred Music: A Journal of Theomusicology* 3, no. 2 (fall 1989).

9. Jon Michael Spencer, *Protest and Praise: Sacred Music of Black Religion* (Minneapolis: Fortress Press, 1990).

10. Garth Baker-Fletcher, *Xodus: An African American Male Journey* (Minneapolis: Fortress Press, 1996).

11. Ibid., 175.

12. Riggins R. Earl Jr., *Dark Symbols, Obscure Signs: God, Self, and Community in the Slave Mind* (Maryknoll, N.Y.: Orbis Books, 1993).

13. Dwight N. Hopkins and George C. L. Cummings, eds., *Cut Loose Your Stammering Tongue: Black Theology in the Slave Narratives* (Maryknoll, N.Y.: Orbis Books, 1991).

14. Dwight N. Hopkins, *Shoes That Fit Our Feet: Sources for a Constructive Black Theology* (Maryknoll, N.Y.: Orbis Books, 1993).

15. Specifically, the three guidelines are: (*a*) God, through Christ, has called humanity to empower the poor; (*b*) a constructive black theology has to rely on its own indigenous sources as foundation but not exclusively; and (*c*) as a hub for a more universal discussion, black theology must begin theological dialogues with Africa and the Third World.

The four relationships entail political and cultural, women and men, Christian and non-Christian, and church and noninstitutional church. Finally, the four types of disciplines out of which a constructive black theology can be developed are political economy, biblical criticism, literary criticism, and comparative religions.

16. Joseph A. Brown, *To Stand on the Rock: Meditations on Black Catholic Identity* (Maryknoll, N.Y.: Orbis Books, 1998).

17. Molefi Kete Asante, a leading scholar of Afrocentricity, defines this movement as "literally, placing African ideals at the center of any analysis that involves African culture and behavior" (Asante, *The Afrocentric Idea* [Philadelphia: Temple University Press, 1987], 6). Other Afrocentric texts are Asante, *Afrocentricity: The Theory of Social Change* (Buffalo, N.Y.: Amulefi, 1980); Cheikh Anta Diop, *Civilization or Barbarism: An Authentic Anthology* (Brooklyn, N.Y.: Lawrence Hill, 1991); idem, *The African Origin of Civilization: Myth or Reality?* (Westport, Conn.: Lawrence Hill, 1974); George G. M. James, *Stolen Legacy: The Greeks Were Not the Authors of Greek Philosophy but the People of North Africa, Commonly Called the Egyptians* (San Francisco: Julian Richardson Associates, 1988); Ivan Van Sertima, ed., *Egypt Revisited* (New Brunswick, N.J.: Transaction Publishers, 1991); Martin Bernal, *Black Athena: The Afroasiatic Roots of Classical Civilization,* vol. 1: *The Fabrication of Ancient Greece 1785– 1985* (New Brunswick, N.J.: Rutgers University Press, 1987); and idem, *Black Athena: The Afroasiatic Roots of Classical Civilization,* vol. 2:

The Archaeological and Documentary Evidence (New Brunswick, N.J.: Rutgers University Press, 1991).

Afrocentricity reached a broad African American audience in the 1980s, particularly with its popularization through the medium of rap songs and a proliferation of Malcolm X books and Malcolm X insignia worn by black inner-city youths and blacks in colleges. In the mid-1980s, Afrocentricity came of age when a group of black church leaders, scholars, activists, and intellectuals (with strong advocacy by Rev. Jesse L. Jackson) "officially" changed black people's name to African American in order to show the direct linkage between black America and Africa.

18. Cain Hope Felder, *Troubling Biblical Waters: Race, Class, and Family* (Maryknoll, N.Y.: Orbis Books, 1989).

19. Walter Brueggemann, in the "Religion" section of *The Atlantic Journal–the Atlanta Constitution,* January 26, 1991.

20. Cain Hope Felder, ed., *Stony the Road We Trod* (Minneapolis: Fortress Press, 1991).

21. Robert Hood, *Must God Remain Greek? Afro Cultures and God-Talk* (Minneapolis: Fortress Press, 1990).

22. Robert Hood, *Begrimed and Black: Christian Traditions on Blacks and Blackness* (Minneapolis: Fortress Press, 1994).

23. Jon Michael Spencer, *Sing a New Song: Liberating Black Hymnody* (Minneapolis: Fortress Press, 1994).

24. Theodore Walker, *Empower the People: Social Ethics for the African-American Church* (Maryknoll, N.Y.: Orbis Books, 1991).

25. Katie G. Cannon, "Hitting a Straight Lick with a Crooked Stick: The Womanist Dilemma in the Development of a Black Liberation Ethic," in *Katie's Canon: Womanism and the Soul of the Black Community,* ed. Katie G. Cannon (New York: Continuum, 1995), 122.

26. Arthur McCray, *The Black Presence in the Bible,* 2 vols. (Chicago: Black Light Fellowship, 1990).

27. Joseph V. Crockett, *Teaching Scripture from an African-American Perspective* (Nashville: Discipleship Resources, 1990).

28. Stephen B. Reid, *Experience and Tradition: A Primer in Black Biblical Hermeneutics* (Nashville: Abingdon Press, 1990).

29. Thomas L. Hoyt Jr., *A Study of the Book of Romans: The Church in Your House* (Hartford, Conn.: Hoyt Publications, 1991).

A second-generation trend of relying on Howard Thurman and Martin Luther King Jr. as sources is seen in Luther Smith, *Howard Thurman: The Mystic as Prophet* (Lanham, Md.: University Press of America, 1981); Mozella Mitchell, *The Spiritual Dynamics of Howard Thurman's Theology* (Bristol, Ind.: Wyndham Hall Press, 1985); Carlyle Stewart, *God, Being, and Liberation: A Comparative Analysis of the Theologies and*

Ethics of James H. Cone and Howard Thurman (Lanham, Md.: University Press of America, 1989); Walter Fluker, *They Look for a City: A Comparative Analysis of the Ideal Community in the Thought of Howard Thurman and Martin Luther King, Jr.* (Lanham, Md.: University Press of America, 1989); Lewis Baldwin, *There Is a Balm in Gilead: The Cultural Roots of Martin Luther King, Jr.* (Minneapolis: Fortress Press, 1991); idem, *To Make the Wounded Whole: The Cultural Legacy of Martin Luther King, Jr.* (Minneapolis: Fortress Press, 1992); and Alton Pollard, *Mysticism and Social Change: Social Witness of Howard Thurman* (New York: Peter Lang, 1992).

30. James H. Evans Jr., *We Have Been Believers: An African American Systematic Theology* (Minneapolis: Fortress Press, 1992). Evans has also applied the method of restructuring traditional disciplines with his more recent practical theology book, *We Shall All Be Changed: Social Problems and Theological Renewal* (Minneapolis: Fortress Press, 1997).

31. Robert M. Franklin, *Liberating Visions: Human Fulfillment and Social Justice in African-American Thought* (Minneapolis: Fortress Press, 1990), 1. Franklin's more recent text is *Another Day's Journey: Black Churches Confronting the American Crisis* (Minneapolis: Fortress Press, 1997). Currently he is the president of the Interdenominational Theological Center in Atlanta.

32. Franklin, *Liberating Visions,* 1.

33. Enoch H. Oglesby, *Born in the Fire: Case Studies in Christian Ethics and Globalization* (New York: Pilgrim Press, 1990).

34. Ibid., 5.

35. Noel L. Erskine, *Decolonizing Theology: A Caribbean Perspective* (Maryknoll, N.Y.: Orbis Books, 1981).

36. Ibid., 118–19.

37. Kortright Davis, *Emancipation Still Comin': Explorations in Caribbean Emancipatory Theology* (Maryknoll, N.Y.: Orbis Books, 1990).

38. Josiah U. Young, *Black and African Theologies: Siblings or Distant Cousins?* (Maryknoll, N.Y.: Orbis Books, 1986).

39. Josiah U. Young, *A Pan-African Theology: Providence and the Legacies of the Ancestors* (Trenton, N.J.: Africa World Press, 1992).

40. Dwight N. Hopkins, *Black Theology USA and South Africa: Politics, Culture, and Liberation* (Maryknoll, N.Y.: Orbis Books, 1989).

41. Simon S. Maimela and Dwight N. Hopkins, *We Are One Voice: Essays on Black Theology in the USA and South Africa* (Johannesburg, South Africa: Skotaville Publishers, 1989).

42. George C. L. Cummings, *A Common Journey: Black Theology (USA) and Latin American Liberation Theology* (Maryknoll, N.Y.: Orbis Books, 1993).

43. Anthony Pinn, *Why Lord? Suffering and Evil in Black Theology* (New York: Continuum, 1995).

44. David Emmanuel Goatley, *Were You There? Godforsakenness in Slave Religion* (Maryknoll, N.Y.: Orbis Books, 1996).

45. Mark L. Chapman, *Christianity on Trial: African-American Religious Thought before and after Black Power* (Maryknoll, N.Y.: Orbis Books, 1996).

46. James Harris, *Pastoral Theology: A Black Church Perspective* (Minneapolis: Fortress Press, 1991).

47. Victor Anderson, *Beyond Ontological Blackness: An Essay on African American Religious Criticism* (New York: Continuum, 1995).

48. Dwight N. Hopkins and Sheila Greeve Davaney, eds., *Changing Conversations: Religious Reflection and Cultural Analysis* (New York: Routledge, 1996).

49. Dwight N. Hopkins, David Batstone, Eduardo Mendieta, and Lois Ann Lorentzen, eds., *Liberation Theologies, Postmodernity, and the Americas* (New York: Routledge, 1997).

50. Ibid., 16.

51. See Will Coleman, "Tribal Talk: Black Theology in Postmodern Configurations," *Theology Today* (April 1993): 69. Coleman was a Ph.D. student in systematic theology at the Graduate Theological Union (Berkeley, California); George C. L. Cummings taught systematic theology at the American Baptist Seminary of the West (Berkeley); James Noel taught American church history at San Francisco Theological Seminary (San Anselmo, California); and I then taught theology at Santa Clara University (Santa Clara, California). Beginning in the fall of 1988, the forum met every week, continuing for roughly three and a half years.

Here is a statement from the early literature of the BT Forum: "The BT Forum has its origins among a group of young African-American scholars located in the Berkeley, California, area. We began meeting weekly during the early Fall of 1988 and have been doing so ever since. Our initial objective was to create an environment where aspiring African-American theologians and religious scholars could share in a need to develop a solid basis for cooperative research and writing. Since then we have sought to engender a think-tank for distilling and disseminating information on African-American religious thought within the academy, the black church, the black community, and the broader society. Currently, our specific objectives are: (1) to contribute to African-American religious thought, (2) to equip and educate institutions in teaching black theology and black religion, (3) to assist the black church in recovering self-understanding of its history as it has and continues to relate to the survival of the black community, and (4) to stimulate dialogue/debate among African-

American religious scholars that is multi-disciplinary, multi-religious, and ecumenical."

52. Coleman, "Tribal Talk," 69.

53. The dean's office at the Graduate Theological Union (Berkeley) funded the retreat (Judith A. Berling was the dean at that time). Letters were sent to several womanist and first- and second-generation theologians. The invitation list was intentionally small because the BT Forum saw this get-together mainly as an intimate intellectual and planning meeting to discuss the future of black and womanist theology. Those who responded favorably to the invitation were James H. Cone, J. Deotis Roberts, Charles H. Long, Jacquelyn Grant, Gayraud S. Wilmore, Kelly Brown, Will Coleman, George C. L. Cummings, and myself. Grant and Wilmore were unable to attend.

A word of appreciation should be given specifically to Dean Berling. She helped the BT Forum hold a public seminar at the Graduate Theological Union on black theology in the slave narratives.

54. The following should be acknowledged for the various conversations we held (at different times) to envision this historic conference on black theology and Cone's *Black Theology and Black Power:* W. Clark Gilpin (dean, University of Chicago Divinity School); J. Timothy Child (associate dean for external relations, University of Chicago Divinity School); Sandra Peppers (administrative staff for Dean Gilpin); Marsha Peeler (my secretary at the Divinity School); Kazi Joshua (my research assistant); Jay Vanasco (media office of the University of Chicago); Martin E. Marty (University of Chicago Divinity School); Michael Dawson (director, Center for the Study of Race, Politics, and Culture at the University of Chicago); and Linda E. Thomas (Garrett-Evangelical Theological Seminary, Evanston, Illinois). I have edited the conference papers in *Black Faith and Public Talk* (Maryknoll, N.Y.: Orbis Books, 1999).

55. James H. Cone, *Martin and Malcolm and America: A Dream or a Nightmare* (Maryknoll, N.Y.: Orbis Books, 1991).

56. C. Eric Lincoln (with Larry H. Mamiya), *The Black Church in the African American Experience* (Durham, N.C.: Duke University Press, 1990).

57. Gayraud S. Wilmore, ed., *African American Religious Studies: An Interdisciplinary Anthology* (Durham, N.C.: Duke University Press, 1989).

58. Gayraud S. Wilmore, ed., *Black Men in Prison: The Response of the African American Church* (Atlanta: ITC Press, 1990); and idem, ed., *Reclamation of Black Prisoners: A Challenge to the African American Church* (Atlanta: ITC Press, 1992).

59. Wilmore, *Black Religion.*

60. Major J. Jones, *The Color of God: The Concept of God in Afro-American Thought* (Macon, Ga.: Mercer University Press, 1987).

61. Charles Shelby Rooks, *Revolution in Zion: Reshaping African American Ministry, 1960–1974* (New York: Pilgrim Press, 1990).

62. Vincent Harding, *Martin Luther King: The Inconvenient Hero* (Maryknoll, N.Y.: Orbis Books, 1996).

63. J. Deotis Roberts, *The Prophethood of Black Believers: An African American Political Theology for Ministry* (Louisville: Westminster/John Knox Press, 1994).

64. Peter J. Paris, *The Spirituality of African Peoples: The Search for a Common Moral Discourse* (Minneapolis: Fortress Press, 1995).

65. Cone and Wilmore, *Black Theology, 1966–1979*; idem, eds., *Black Theology: A Documentary History, 1980–1992* (Maryknoll, N.Y.: Orbis Books, 1993).

66. Many of the second generation have received research grants, accepted positions at Ph.D.-granting institutions, and institutionalized their discipline in the American Academy of Religion. For instance, the womanist program unit in the AAR and the black biblical scholars program unit in the Society of Biblical Literature have been leading intellectual gatherings. I chaired the first seven years of the black theology program unit in the American Academy of Religion. Will Coleman is the current chair. Similarly, second-generation theologians are editors of the black religious series at various publishing houses. For instance, Cheryl Kirk Duggan, Anthony Pinn, Karen Baker-Fletcher, and Garth Baker-Fletcher work in these roles, and I am the editor of the Henry McNeal Turner—Sojourner Truth Series on Black Religion for Orbis Books.

67. Karen Baker-Fletcher and Garth Baker-Fletcher, *My Sister, My Brother: Womanist and Xodus God-Talk* (Maryknoll, N.Y.: Orbis Books, 1997).

4. Womanist Theology

1. "The Special Plight and the Role of Black Women" was a speech given by Hamer at the NAACP Legal Defense Fund Institute, New York City, May 7, 1991. The text can be found in Gerda Lerner, ed., *Black Women in White America: A Documentary History* (New York: Vintage Books, 1973), 609–13.

2. Deborah Gray White, *Ar'n't I a Woman? Female Slaves in the Plantation South* (New York: W. W. Norton, 1985), 124.

3. Alice Walker, *In Search of Our Mothers' Gardens: Womanist Prose* (New York: Harcourt Brace Jovanovich, 1983).

4. Ibid., xi–xii.

5. Some of the struggles facing black women in the 1960s are discussed in Jacqueline Jones, *Labor of Love, Labor of Sorrow: Black Women, Work, and the Family, from Slavery to the Present* (New York: Vintage Books, 1986).

6. Jacquelyn Grant, "Black Theology and the Black Woman," in *Black Theology: A Documentary History, 1966–1979,* ed. Gayraud S. Wilmore and James H. Cone (Maryknoll, N.Y.: Orbis Books, 1979), 423.

7. Katie G. Cannon, "The Emergence of Black Feminist Consciousness," in *Feminist Interpretation of the Bible,* ed. Letty M. Russell (Louisville: Westminster Press, 1985), 40.

8. Williams's article, "Womanist Theology: Black Women's Voices," can be found in *Black Theology: A Documentary History, 1980–1992,* ed. James H. Cone and Gayraud S. Wilmore (Maryknoll, N.Y.: Orbis Books, 1993).

9. Linda E. Thomas, "Womanist Theology, Epistemology, and a New Anthropological Paradigm," *Cross Currents* 48, no. 4 (winter/spring 1998-1999): 492.

10. Williams, "Womanist Theology," 269.

11. Kelly Brown Douglas, *The Black Christ* (Maryknoll, N.Y.: Orbis Books, 1994), 114.

12. Ibid.

13. Thomas, "Womanist Theology," 488–99.

14. Ibid. Thomas is a professor of theology and anthropology at Garrett-Evangelical Theological Seminary in Evanston, Illinois, where she is doing a comparative study of poor black Christian women in South Side Chicago and those in townships in South Africa. As an anthropologist who practices Christianity, she combines the commitment of her Christian witness (she is an ordained United Methodist clergywoman) with the scientific ethnographic techniques of fieldwork.
In the above-quoted article she elaborates the specific steps womanists need to follow to actually be with poor black women in their communities and churches.

15. Emilie M. Townes, introduction to *A Troubling in My Soul: Womanist Perspectives on Evil and Suffering,* ed. Emilie M. Townes (Maryknoll, N.Y.: Orbis Books, 1993), 2.

16. Teresa L. Fry, "Avoiding Asphyxiation: A Womanist Perspective on Intrapersonal and Interpersonal Transformation," in *Embracing the Spirit: Womanist Perspectives on Hope, Salvation, and Transformation,* ed. Emilie M. Townes (Maryknoll, N.Y.: Orbis Books, 1997), chap. 6. All references to Fry's work are from this article.

17. Katie G. Cannon, *Black Womanist Ethics* (Atlanta: Scholars Press, 1988), 4.

18. Katie G. Cannon, ed., *Katie's Canon: Womanism and the Soul of the Black Community* (New York: Continuum, 1995), 61.

19. Ibid., 25.

20. Ibid., 70.

21. Ibid., 146.

22. Renita J. Weems, *Just a Sister Away: A Womanist Vision of Women's Relationships in the Bible* (San Diego: LuraMedia, 1988).

23. Ibid., 17.

24. Ibid., 30.

25. Renita J. Weems, *Battered Love: Marriage, Sex, and Violence in the Hebrew Prophets* (Minneapolis: Augsburg Fortress, 1995), xiii.

26. Ibid., 1–2.

27. Jacquelyn Grant, *White Women's Christ and Black Women's Jesus: Feminist Christology and Womanist Response* (Atlanta: Scholars Press, 1989).

28. Ibid., 217.

29. Ibid., 220.

30. See Grant's article "Womanist Jesus and the Mutual Struggle for Liberation," in *The Recovery of Black Presence: An Interdisciplinary Exploration,* ed. Randall C. Bailey and Jacquelyn Grant (Nashville: Abingdon, 1995), 129–42.

31. Ibid., 137.

32. Delores S. Williams, *Sisters in the Wilderness: The Challenge of Womanist God-Talk* (Maryknoll, N.Y.: Orbis Books, 1993).

33. Ibid., 6.

34. Emilie M. Townes, *Womanist Justice, Womanist Hope* (Atlanta: Scholars Press, 1993).

35. Ibid., 1–2.

36. Emilie M. Townes, *In a Blaze of Glory: Womanist Spirituality as Social Witness* (Nashville: Abingdon, 1995).

37. Ibid., 13, 11.

38. Townes, *Troubling;* idem, *Embracing the Spirit.* Another important source for developing a womanist theology and ethics is Bettye Collier-Thomas, ed., *Daughters of Thunder: Black Women Preachers and Their Sermons, 1850–1979* (San Francisco: Jossey-Bass Publishers, 1998); the book includes thirty-eight sermons by black women that had never been previously published.

39. Douglas, *Black Christ,* 24.

40. Ibid., 98.

41. Ibid., 109–10.

42. Karen Baker-Fletcher, *A Singing Something: Womanist Reflections on Anna Julia Cooper* (New York: Crossroad, 1994), 15.

43. Marcia Y. Riggs, *Awake, Arise, and Act: A Womanist Call for Black Liberation* (Cleveland: Pilgrim Press, 1994), 1.

44. Ibid., 10–11.

45. Ibid., 80.

46. Ibid., 82.

47. Ibid., 12.

48. Two pioneering books on womanist perspectives on ecology and music are Karen Baker-Fletcher, *Sisters of Dust, Sisters of Spirit: A Creation-Centered Womanist Spirituality* (Minneapolis: Fortress Press, 1998); and Cheryl A. Kirk-Duggan, *Exorcizing Evil: A Womanist Perspective on the Spirituals* (Maryknoll, N.Y.: Orbis Books, 1997).

In the area of a Roman Catholic examination of womanist theology, see Diana L. Hayes, *Hagar's Daughters: Womanist Ways of Being in the World* (New York: Paulist Press, 1995); and idem, *And Still We Rise: An Introduction to Black Liberation Theology* (New York: Paulist Press, 1996). A former lawyer, Hayes received her Ph.D. from the Catholic University of Louvain and was the first African American woman to earn an S.T.D. there. She is associate professor of theology at Georgetown University and serves as an adjunct faculty member for the Master of Theology in Black Catholic Studies program at Xavier University, New Orleans.

5. Black Theology and Third World Liberation Theologies

1. Martin Luther King Jr., *The Trumpet of Conscience* (New York: Harper and Row, 1967), 62.

2. In James M. Washington, ed., *A Testament of Hope: The Essential Writings and Speeches of Martin Luther King Jr.* (San Francisco: HarperCollins, 1986), 364.

3. "At the Audubon," in *Malcolm X Speaks: Selected Speeches and Statements*, ed. George Breitman (New York: Grove Press, 1966), 125.

4. The two representatives were J. Metz Rollins, then executive director of NCNC, and Gayraud S. Wilmore, then the chair of NCNC's theological commission. For the history of black theology's relation to African theology see Gayraud S. Wilmore, "The Role of Afro-America in the Rise of Third World Theology: A Historical Reappraisal," in *African Theology en Route,* ed. Kofi Appiah-Kubi and Sergio Torres (Maryknoll, N.Y.: Orbis Books, 1979).

5. Papers from this meeting are found in Priscilla Massie, ed., *Black Faith and Black Solidarity: Pan-Africanism and Faith in Christ* (New York: Friendship Press, 1973). For relevant commentary and analyses,

see Cornish Rogers, "Pan-Africanism and the Black Church: A Search for Solidarity," *Christian Century,* November 17, 1971; E. E. Mshana, "The Challenge of Black Theology and African Theology," *Africa Theological Journal* 5 (December 1975).

6. For the papers from this gathering, see the *Journal of Religious Thought* 32, no. 2 (fall–winter 1975). For important commentary, see James H. Cone, "Black and African Theologies: A Consultation," *Christianity and Crisis* 35, no. 3, March 3, 1975; and Gayraud S. Wilmore, "To Speak with One Voice? The Ghana Consultation on African and Black Theology," *Christian Century,* February 19, 1975.

7. Papers from the December Accra meeting are found in Appiah-Kubi and Torres, *African Theology en Route.* Also see Gayraud S. Wilmore, "Theological Ferment in the Third World," *Christian Century,* February 17, 1978.

8. The papers were published in Simon S. Maimela and Dwight N. Hopkins, eds., *We Are One Voice: Black Theology in the USA and South Africa* (Johannesburg: Skotaville Publishers, 1989).

9. Some of the South African presenters were Simon S. Maimela and Itumeleng J. Mosala; some of the American lecturers were Jacquelyn Grant, Randy Bailey, and myself.

10. For primary documents and extended analyses of African theology and black theology, see Appiah-Kubi and Torres, *African Theology en Route;* Josiah U. Young, *Black and African Theologies: Siblings or Distant Cousins?* (Maryknoll, N.Y.: Orbis Books, 1986); Dwight N. Hopkins, *Black Theology USA and South Africa: Politics, Culture, and Liberation* (Maryknoll N.Y.: Orbis Books, 1989); and Emmanuel Martey, *African Theology: Inculturation and Liberation* (Maryknoll, N.Y.: Orbis Books, 1993).

11. James H. Cone, *Black Theology and Black Power* (Maryknoll, N.Y.: Orbis Books, 1997). The book was part of the international intellectual trends that went into the political and cultural formation of the black consciousness movement and black theology in South Africa. See also Steve Biko, *Steve Biko: I Write What I Like,* ed. Aelred Stubbs (San Francisco: Harper and Row, 1986); Gail Gerhart, *Black Power in South Africa: The Evolution of an Ideology* (Berkeley: University of California Press, 1979); Robert Fatton Jr., *Black Consciousness in South Africa* (Albany: State University of New York Press, 1986); and Ernest Harsch, *South Africa: White Rule Black Revolt* (New York: Monad Press, 1983).

12. See Gabriel M. Setiloane, *African Theology: An Introduction* (Johannesburg: Skotaville Publishers, 1986).

For fuller interpretations of how black theology developed in relation to African theology, see James H. Cone, "The Future and ... African Theology," *Pro Veritate*, January 15, and February 15, 1972; John Mbiti, "An African Views American Black Theology," *Worldview* 17 (August 1974); Desmond M. Tutu, "Black Theology/African Theology — Soul Mates Or Antagonists?" *Journal of Religious Thought* 32, no. 1 (fall–winter 1975); James H. Cone, "A Black American Perspective on the Future of African Theology," in *Black Theology: A Documentary History, 1966–1979*, ed. Gayraud S. Wilmore and James H. Cone (Maryknoll, N.Y.: Orbis Books, 1979); and J. Deotis Roberts, "An Afro-American/African Theological Dialogue," in *Black Theology in Dialogue* (Philadelphia: Westminster Press, 1987).

13. For French-speaking Africans and those outside of South Africa working with the idea of liberation, see the publications of Englebert Mveng and the books of Jean-Marc Ela, *African Cry* (Maryknoll, N.Y: Orbis Books, 1986), and *My Faith as an African* (Maryknoll, N.Y.: Orbis Books, 1986).

14. For accounts of the dialogue between black theology in the United States and Latin American theology, see James H. Cone, "From Geneva to São Paulo: A Dialogue between Black Theology and Latin American Liberation Theology," in *The Challenge of Basic Christian Communities*, ed. Sergio Torres and John Eagleson (Maryknoll, N.Y.: Orbis Books, 1981); and George C. L. Cummings, *A Common Journey: Black Theology (USA) and Latin American Liberation Theology* (Maryknoll, N.Y.: Orbis Books, 1993).

15. Gustavo Gutiérrez, *A Theology of Liberation* (Maryknoll, N.Y.: Orbis Books, 1973); the original Spanish edition was published in 1971.

16. Cone, *Black Theology and Black Power*; idem, *A Black Theology of Liberation*, 2d ed. (Maryknoll, N.Y.: Orbis Books, 1986).

17. Translated by Manuel Mercader and published by Carlos Lohlé, Calle Tacuari 1516, Buenos Aires.

18. Regarding this dialogue, see *Risk* 9, no. 2 (1973).

19. The book on the conference is Sergio Torres and John Eagleson, eds., *Theology in the Americas* (Maryknoll, N.Y.: Orbis Books, 1976).

20. See Cone, "From Geneva to São Paulo."

21. Cone's lecture appears as "Fe cristiana y praxis política," in *Praxis cristiana y producción teológica*, ed. Jorge V. Pixley and Jean-Pierre Bastian (Salamanca: Sígueme, 1979).

22. James H. Cone, "A Black American Perspective on the Asian Search for a Full Humanity," in *Asia's Struggle for Full Humanity*, ed. Virginia Fabella (Maryknoll, N.Y.: Orbis Books, 1980), 179. For another black theologian's comments on the dialogue, see J. Deotis Roberts, "Black Theology in Dialogue: Two Examples," in *Black Theology in Dialogue* (Philadelphia: Westminster Press, 1987).

23. For Cone's report on and interpretation of this conference, see his "'Asia's Struggle for a Full Humanity: Toward a Relevant Theology' (An Asian Theological Conference)," in Wilmore and Cone, *Black Theology, 1966–1979*, 593–601.

24. On the origin of EATWOT, see Oscar K. Bimwenyi, "A l'origine de l'association oecumenique des theologiens du tiers monde," in *Bulletin de Theologie Africaine* 2, no. 3 (January–June 1980); James H. Cone, "Ecumenical Association of Third World Theologians," *Ecumenical Trends* 14, no. 8 (September 1985); and Sergio Torres, "Dar es Salaam 1976," in *Theologies of the Third World: Convergences and Differences*, ed. Leonardo Boff and Virgil Elizondo (Edinburgh: T. and T. Clark, 1988), 105–15.

25. Important books on Third World women in the development of liberation theology are Musimbi R. A. Kanyoro and Nyambura J. Njoroge, eds., *Groaning in Faith: African Women in the Household of God* (Nairobi: Action Publishers, 1996); Mercy Amba Oduyoye and Musimbi R. A. Kanyoro, eds., *The Will to Arise: Women, Tradition, and the Church in Africa* (Maryknoll, N.Y.: Orbis Books, 1992); Virginia Fabella and Sun Ai Lee Park, eds., *We Dare to Dream: Doing Theology as Asian Women* (Hong Kong: Asian Women's Resource Center for Culture and Theology, 1989); Elsa Tamez, ed., *Through Her Eyes: Women's Theology from Latin America* (Maryknoll, N.Y.: Orbis Books, 1989); Maria Pilar Aquino, ed., *Our Cry for Life: Feminist Theology from Latin America* (Maryknoll, N.Y.: Orbis Books, 1993); Mary John Mananzan et al., eds., *Women Resisting Violence: Spirituality for Life* (Maryknoll, N.Y.: Orbis Books, 1996); John S. Pobee and Barbel Von Wartenberg-Potter, eds., *New Eyes for Reading: Biblical and Theological Reflections by Women from the Third World* (Geneva: World Council of Churches, 1986); Virginia Fabella and Dolorita Martínez, eds., *The Oaxtepec Encounter: Third World Women Doing Theology* (Port Harcourt, Nigeria: EATWOT [P.O. Box 499, Port Harcourt, Nigeria, 1987]); Virginia Fabella and Mercy Amba Oduyoye, eds., *With Passion and Compassion: Third World Women Doing Theology* (Maryknoll, N.Y.: Orbis Books, 1988); and Ursula King, ed., *Feminist Theology from the Third World: A Reader* (Maryknoll, N.Y.: Orbis Books, 1994).

26. EATWOT has held various meetings since it began in Dar es Salaam in 1976. Some of its proceedings and papers are found in the following: Sergio Torres and Virginia Fabella, eds., *The Emergent Gospel: Theology from the Underside of History* (Maryknoll, N.Y.: Orbis Books, 1978); Appiah-Kubi and Torres, *African Theology en Route;* Fabella, *Asia's Struggle for Full Humanity;* Torres and Eagleson, *Challenge of Basic Christian Communities;* Virginia Fabella and Sergio Torres, eds., *Irruption of the Third World: Challenge to Theology* (Maryknoll, N.Y.:

Orbis Books, 1983); Virginia Fabella and Sergio Torres, eds., *Doing Theology in a Divided World* (Maryknoll, N.Y.: Orbis Books, 1985); Boff and Elizondo, *Theologies of the Third World;* and K. C. Abraham, ed., *Third World Theologies: Commonalities and Divergences* (Maryknoll, N.Y.: Orbis Books, 1990).

6. Conclusion

1. For instance, James H. Cone has been a past chair of the association's theological commission, and I became the chair after Cone.

2. See Gayraud S. Wilmore and James H. Cone, eds., *Black Theology: A Documentary History, 1966–1979* (Maryknoll, N.Y.: Orbis Books, 1979), 38.

Index

225

Index

226

Begrimed and Black: Christian Traditions on Blacks and Blackness (Hood), 96

Beloved (Morrison), 149

ben-Jochannan, Yosef A., 97

Bernal, Martin, 97

Beyond Ontological Blackness: An Essay on African American Religious Criticism (Anderson), 110

Bible, the: black homosexuals and, 199; the development of black theology and, 23–28; Long on, 79; points of agreement of all liberation theologies on, 178; second-generation scholars' reinterpretation of, 98–99; slaves and, 21–22, 163; as a source of black theology, 42–43; synopsis of black theology's relation to, 183; and the theft of Africa's resources, 164; womanist theology on women in, 140–43

biblical scholars: challenges to objectivity of white, 95; emphases of second-generation, 98–99; womanist, 140–43, 146–47. *See also* Bible, the

Biko, Steve, 52

Bimwenyi, Abbe Oscar K., 176

Bingemer, Maria Clara, 112

Black and African Theologies: Siblings or Distant Cousins? (Young), 104

The Black Christ (Douglas), 149–52

black church, the: the academy and, 11–12; black theology's relation to, 4–6; the civil rights movement and, 33–34; current challenges to, 196–202; first-

generation black theologians and, 122; Lincoln's research on, 117–18; the political wing of black theology and, 187; Roberts on, 119–20; as a source of black theology, 43–44; Washington (Joseph R.) on, 30–32; Wilmore on, 68; womanist theology and, 135, 147–48, 150; women as the foundation of, 128

The Black Church in the African American Experience (Lincoln), 117–18

black clergy, the: black power movement and, 37–38, 39–40; the civil rights movement and, 34; Wilmore on, 69–70; women and, 197–98

black consciousness movement, 52

black English, 44, 45, 90

"Black Identity and Solidarity and the Role of the Church as a Medium for Social Change" (conference), 160

black Judaism, 69, 79

Black Men in Prison: The Response of the African American Church (Wilmore), 118

black Messiah, the, 63, 64, 207n.11, 207n.12

black Muslims/black Islam, 40, 69, 79

black nationalism, 36, 39, 151, 159

blackness: Anderson on, 110; Biko on, 52; the black power movement on, 184; Cone on, 55, 57–58; first-generation black theology and, 50–51; God and, 166; Hood on, 96; Malcolm X on, 37; need for the church to affirm, 199–200